THE HEALTHY GOURMET

THE HEALTHY GOURMET

BY
PATRICIA HAUSMAN AND
JUDITH BENN HURLEY

NAL BOOKS

NEW AMERICAN LIBRARY

A DIVISION OF PENGUIN BOOKS USA INC., NEW YORK
PUBLISHED IN CANADA BY
PENGUIN BOOKS CANADA LIMITED, MARKHAM, ONTARIO

Copyright © 1989 by Patricia Hausman and Judith Benn Hurley

All rights reserved. For information address New American Library.

Published simultaneously in Canada by Penguin Books Canada Limited

 NAL BOOKS TRADEMARK REG. U.S. PAT. OFF. AND FOREIGN COUNTRIES
REGISTERED TRADEMARK — MARCA REGISTRADA
HECHO EN BRATTLEBORO, VT, U.S.A.

SIGNET, SIGNET CLASSIC, MENTOR, ONYX, PLUME, MERIDIAN and
NAL BOOKS are published in the United States by New American Library,
a division of Penguin Books USA Inc., 1633 Broadway, New York, New York
10019, in Canada by Penguin Books Canada Limited, 2801 John Street,
Markham, Ontario L3R 1B4

Library of Congress Cataloging-in-Publication Data

Hausman, Patricia.
    The healthy gourmet / by Patricia Hausman and Judith Benn Hurley.
        p.   cm.
    ISBN 0-453-00692-2
    1. Quick and easy cookery. 2. Reducing diets — Recipes.
3. Microwave cookery. 4. Menus.   I. Hurley, Judith Benn.
II. Title.
TX833.5.H38   1989
641.5′55 — dc20   89-12873
                                                                                                CIP

Designed by Leonard Telesca

First Printing, November, 1989

1   2   3   4   5   6   7   8   9

For Glenn and for Patrick

Contents

Introduction

Whether you live to eat or eat to live, *The Healthy Gourmet* has the recipes for you.

One of us is a nutritionist, the other a professional chef. We're both convinced that making nutritious foods delicious is the key to better health. Knowledge of nutrition rarely goes far, we've found, unless the foods that make for healthful eating are prepared in a way that tastes great.

That once seemed like a tall order to us, but not anymore. After thousands of hours of experimenting, we've found ways to make good nutrition taste better than ever before. This book is the result.

Naturally, our recipes focus on today's top issues: getting more fiber and complex carbohydrates on the menu while reducing calories, fat, salt, and sugar. To do this yet maintain flavor, we've worked hard to uncover the principles of maximizing taste and nutrition. Using our secrets, you can learn entirely new approaches to cooking that will:

- keep lean meats moist and tender
- turn everyday foods like cottage cheese into blue-ribbon cheesecakes, pancakes, and dips
- make flavoring foods with lots of unwholesome ingredients totally unnecessary. Thanks to clever blends of herbs and

spices, lively combinations of fruits and vegetables, and fresh, tasty ingredients, you can say good-bye to recipes that rely heavily on fat, salt, or sugar for flavoring food.

Each of the ten chapters of *The Healthy Gourmet* focuses on a specific type of food. Within the recipe chapters, you'll find dozens of secrets explained, then illustrated with a recipe or two. In addition to providing enjoyable recipes, we encourage you to use these secrets to modify your own favorites. You'll find that almost any recipe can be made more healthful. All it takes to make it so is your own ingenuity and, of course, the right secrets.

— Patricia Hausman and
Judith Benn Hurley

THE
HEALTHY
GOURMET

Bread and Breakfasts

Recently a young woman wrote in complete despair over her whole-grain bread baking. She wanted to bake tasty, wholesome high-fiber loaves for her family but wound up with bread that had a gummy texture, flat taste, and resembled bricks. Most people who experience these problems — and there are quite a few — give up baking entirely. But if you've had similar problems, don't abandon the healthful benefits of homemade bread — help is at hand.

The first thing to do is to be sure you're using bread flour. This advice may sound ridiculous until you realize that there are other types of flour and that no labeling is required on packages. Bread, or hard wheat, flour has a higher gluten content than other flours and will help your whole-grain loaves rise to their full potential. To guarantee you're getting bread flour, buy it from a reputable store or go to a mill. This seems like a lot of trouble, but it's the best way to get flour consistent in quality. Besides being inadequately labeled, flour from many stores may sit too long in adverse conditions; whole-grain flour becomes rancid faster than white flour and shouldn't be stored for longer than six months. If you don't know of a reputable mill, contact Great Valley Mills, 687 Mill Road, Telford, PA 18969.

The next important step is to explore the bread recipes in this chapter. They're easy, delicious, and high in fiber, B vitamins, and other nutrients. Orange Marmalade Bread can be prepared in less than an hour; Chive and Cheddar Scones make great snacks, appetizers, or accompaniments; and Pinto Bean Bread gives the common bean its most uncommon use ever.

Most breads, of course, make great toast—but don't stop at the bread if you're looking for a delicious, nutritious breakfast. We'll show you how to slash fat, calories, and cholesterol from omelettes and scrambled eggs. You'll learn to prepare whole-grain pancakes and waffles that are light in fat as well as texture. If you're a cereal eater, we'll acquaint you with a slew of new, healthful ways to enjoy it. If you don't like to eat breakfast first thing in the morning, you'll welcome a few secrets on how to meet that challenge. Many of the recipes are portable, so you can take them to work with you and enjoy them mid-morning or when you're in the mood.

Many people wouldn't dream of skipping breakfast, and we agree. In our view, the morning is the perfect time to eat because your taste buds are at their freshest and most alert. Since you've been without food for hours, whole grains taste extra nutty and rich and the true essence of fruit is perceivable —no fat or sugar needed. When you try your first recipe from this chapter, spend a moment really thinking about what you're tasting and your day will be off to a sensational start.

The Yolk's on You

If you've been using whole eggs in omelettes and scrambled eggs, cut down on fat, calories, and cholesterol by substituting egg whites for all but one whole egg. When combined with the right ingredients and beaten until bubbly, the results are just as tasty and tender as when whole eggs are used.

ENLIGHTENED OMELETTE

2 SERVINGS

Delicious with whole-grain toast and chilled orange sections.

> 1 egg
> 2 egg whites
> 2 teaspoons water
> 2 teaspoons canola or other vegetable oil
> ¼ teaspoon dijon-style mustard
> splash hot pepper sauce

Combine all of the ingredients in a medium bowl and whisk until bubbly and creamy looking, about 1 minute.

Spray a 10-inch nonstick pan with nonstick vegetable spray and heat on medium-high. Pour in the egg mixture and swirl the pan a bit for even cooking. If you're adding a filling, do so now.

Continue to cook and swirl until the egg mixture is set, about 2½ to 3 minutes.

Use a spatula to coax the edges of the omelette from the pan, then tip the omelette onto a plate, folding it over as you go. Serve warm.

Ideas for Omelette Fillings

Sprinkle ¼ cup of any of the following onto an omelette before it sets.

- Chopped tomato and grated reduced-fat cheddar cheese
- Minced shallot and chopped smoked salmon
- Sliced pear and Neufchatel or reduced-fat cream cheese
- Leftover stir-fried vegetables
- Chopped olives and minced scallions

The Water Method

Instead of using milk or cream in omelettes and scrambled eggs, use water. Water not only reduces fat and calories, but actually makes the finished product fluffier.

EGG SCRAMBLE

1 SERVING

Accompany this scramble with a whole-grain muffin, or stuff into a halved pita with a sprinkle of chives and some lowfat cottage cheese.

> 2 egg whites
> 1 teaspoon water
> 1 teaspoon canola oil
> ¼ teaspoon prepared dijon-style mustard

Combine all of the ingredients in a medium bowl and whisk until bubbly.

Spray a nonstick pan with nonstick vegetable spray and heat on medium-high. Pour in the egg mixture and use a wooden spatula to turn and flip while it cooks. The scramble is done when it's firm, about 1 minute. Take care not to overcook or the texture will be rubbery. Serve warm.

Halt the Salt

Buy salt-free dairy products, then add salt to taste if you find it necessary. Certain brands of cheese, such as salt-free cottage cheese, are tasty enough that you may find you need no salt at all.

CORN BREAD PUDDING WITH JALAPEÑO

6 SERVINGS

2 cups (about 6 ounces) coarsely crumbled corn bread
⅓ cup (about 1½ ounces) shredded lowfat Monterey Jack
*   cheese with jalapeño*
1 egg
1 egg white
½ cup lowfat cottage cheese or part-skim ricotta
1 cup skim milk

Preheat the oven to 400°F. Spray a 9-inch glass pie dish with nonstick vegetable spray. Then toss in the corn bread and Jack cheese.

Put the egg, egg white, cottage cheese, and milk in a blender and whiz until combined. Pour the mixture over the corn bread.

Bake on center rack of oven until firm, about 25 to 30 minutes. Serve warm for brunch. Great with sliced ripe tomato or roasted sweet peppers.

A Juicy Idea

Whole-grain bread won't soak up milk evenly. So, when making French toast, use juice instead. Apple or cranberry are favorites for this.

ENGLISH MUFFIN FRENCH TOAST

4 SERVINGS

1 egg
1 egg white
¼ cup apricot nectar or apple juice
½ teaspoon vanilla
4 whole wheat English muffins, split
applesauce for serving

Combine the egg and egg white in a medium bowl and whisk until lemony in color. Then pour in the nectar and vanilla and whisk until combined. Soak the muffin halves in the mixture for about 5 minutes.

Meanwhile, spray a nonstick pan with nonstick vegetable spray and heat on medium-high. Set each muffin half in the pan and press with a spatula so the insides cook. Continue to press and cook until burnished, then flip and continue to cook as before. The muffins will take about 2½ minutes per side. (If you have to cook the muffins in batches, keep the cooked ones covered in foil in a warm oven.) Serve warm with applesauce.

Flour Power

Since heat, cold, weather, and age affect flour, always try to weigh rather than measure it. Also note that whole wheat pastry flour is best for pancakes, waffles, and pastries because its low gluten content won't make them gummy.

COTTAGE CHEESE PANCAKES WITH FRESH FRUIT

4 SERVINGS

2 ounces (about ½ cup) whole wheat pastry flour
2½ ounces (about ½ cup) unbleached flour
½ cup wheat germ
½ teaspoon baking powder
½ teaspoon baking soda
1 tablespoon maple syrup
1¼ cup skim milk
1 egg
½ cup lowfat cottage cheese
blueberries or other fresh fruit for serving

In a large bowl combine the flours, wheat germ, baking powder, and baking soda.

Pour the maple syrup, milk, egg, and cottage cheese in a blender and whiz until smooth. Then add the dry ingredients and use a large rubber spatula to combine well. Don't overmix.

Spray a nonstick pan with nonstick vegetable spray and heat on medium. For each pancake, drop 2 tablespoons of batter into the pan. When the underside is golden brown, about 2 to 3 minutes, flip and brown the other side. Serve warm, accompanied by blueberries or other fresh fruit.

Butter It Up

Buttermilk, contrary to its name, is usually low in fat. Using it as the liquid in whole-grain baked goods helps keep textures tender. Choose it as an ounce-for-ounce substitute for other liquids.

RAISIN-ORANGE BUTTERMILK OATCAKES

4 SERVINGS

2 ounces (about ¾ cup) rolled oats
1½ cups buttermilk
1½ ounces (about ¼ cup) unbleached flour
1 ounce (about ¼ cup) whole wheat pastry flour
1 egg, beaten
½ teaspoon vanilla
½ teaspoon grated orange zest
2 tablespoons raisins
½ teaspoon baking soda
1 tablespoon molasses

Combine the oats and buttermilk in a large bowl and let soak for about 3 minutes. Add the remaining ingredients and use a large rubber spatula to stir until well combined. Don't overmix.

Spray a nonstick pan with nonstick vegetable spray and heat on medium. For each oatcake, drop about 3 tablespoons of batter into the pan and let cook until bubbles appear on top, about 3 minutes. Then flip and repeat for about 3 minutes more. Serve warm.

Sweet Savvy

Boost nutrition by using fruit juice and all-fruit (no-sugar-added) preserves as sweeteners instead of sugar. Apple and white grape juice are especially compatible with breakfast foods. For instance, stir a tablespoon of apple jelly into a bowl of hot oatmeal.

PEACH-VANILLA PANCAKES WITH HOT PEACH SAUCE

4 SERVINGS

Pancakes:

4 ounces (about 1 cup) whole wheat pastry flour
1½ teaspoons baking powder
2 tablespoons wheat germ
2 tablespoons all-fruit peach preserves
½ teaspoon vanilla
1 egg, beaten
1 cup skim milk
½ cup (about 1 pitted peach) finely chopped fresh peach

In a medium bowl combine the flour, baking powder, and wheat germ.

In another medium bowl combine the preserves, vanilla, egg, milk, and peach. Scoop into the dry ingredients and use a large rubber spatula to combine well. Don't overmix.

Spray a nonstick pan with nonstick vegetable spray and heat on medium. For each pancake drop in about 2 tablespoons of batter and cook until bubbles appear on top, about 3 minutes. Then flip and cook for about 3 minutes more.

Wrap the pancakes in foil and keep them in a warm oven (200°F.) while you prepare the sauce.

Sauce:

½ pound ripe (about 2) peaches
¼ cup white grape juice
¼ teaspoon freshly grated nutmeg

Use a sharp paring knife to peel the peaches. Pit and chop them, then tip into a processor or blender with the juice and whiz until smooth.

Pour into a small saucepan, add the nutmeg, and heat on medium until warm and slightly thickened, about 2 to 3 minutes. Serve warm with Peach-Vanilla Pancakes.

Be a Waffle Whiz

Most health-conscious cooks merely dream of eating waffles. But thanks to the addition of yeast, we can all enjoy waffles that are delicious and lower in fat.

LIGHT AND TENDER WAFFLES

6 SERVINGS

Good with sliced pears or Hot Peach Sauce (page 9).

1 cup skim milk
2 tablespoons sweet butter or margarine
2 tablespoons maple syrup
1½ cups water
1 package dry yeast
2 eggs, beaten
7½ ounces (about 1½ cups) unbleached flour
6 ounces (about 1½ cups) whole wheat pastry flour

Heat the milk over medium heat in a small saucepan until tiny bubbles appear around the edges. Add the butter and stir until dissolved. Remove from heat.

Pour the mixture into a large bowl and add the maple syrup and water. Check to be sure the mixture's warm — about 110°F. If not, heat it. Add the yeast and stir until combined. Then stir in the eggs and flours and use a large wooden spatula to combine.

Let the batter sit, uncovered, until bubbles have begun to form on the surface — about 25 minutes.

Spray the waffle iron molds with nonstick vegetable spray and bake the waffles according to manufacturer's instructions, which will probably be about 4 to 4½ minutes. Serve warm.

EASY BREAKFAST BARS

8 SERVINGS

2 tablespoons canola or safflower oil
¼ cup orange juice concentrate
¼ cup maple syrup
2 cups lightly crushed bran flake cereal
    (with or without raisins)
¼ cup chopped pecans

Preheat oven to 350°F.

Combine the oil, concentrate, and maple syrup in a small saucepan. Over medium heat bring to a boil, stirring constantly. Remove from heat.

Combine the cereal and pecans in a medium bowl and pour in the syrup mixture. Toss until all the pieces are coated with syrup.

Line an 8 x 8-inch baking dish with parchment paper and spray with nonstick vegetable spray. Press in the mixture and bake until firm, about 15 minutes.

Let the bars cool in the refrigerator for about 25 minutes. Then lift from the baking dish, peel off the parchment, and use a kitchen shears to cut into 2 x 4-inch bars. This is a good portable finger food for commuters.

SWISS MIXED BREAKFAST SUNDAE (MUESLI)

4 SERVINGS

2 cups plain lowfat yogurt
1 tablespoon oat bran
1 tablespoon rolled oats
1 tablespoon wheat bran
2 tablespoons finely chopped dried cherries or raisins
½ cup chopped fresh pineapple
½ cup small seedless grapes

In a large bowl mix together the yogurt, oat bran, rolled oats, and wheat bran. Fold in the cherries and pineapple. Cover and refrigerate overnight.

When you're ready, fold in the grapes and serve slightly chilled.

A Hot Idea

 Add extra calcium to your diet by cooking hot cereals in skim milk instead of water.

Friendly Flakes

Keep flaked whole grains — such as rice, wheat, and rye — on hand for quick, nutritious breakfasts. Not to be confused with cold cereal flakes, these are whole grains that have been flattened for speedy cooking but with the bran left intact. (Whole flaked brown rice takes only about 12 minutes to cook as opposed to regular brown rice, which can take 45 minutes.) The texture is cereallike — just perfect for breakfast.

MAKE-YOUR-OWN HOT CEREAL MIX

MAKES ENOUGH FOR 14 SERVINGS

1 cup whole wheat or white couscous
1 cup oat bran
1 cup coarsely chopped flaked brown rice
½ cup dried currants

Combine all of the ingredients in a large jar; then cover and refrigerate.

To make cereal for one, combine 1 cup of cool water or skim milk and 1 cup of cereal mix in a small saucepan and combine well. Gradually bring it to a boil over high heat. Then reduce the heat and simmer until the liquid has been absorbed (about 5 minutes), stirring frequently. Serve hot.

Dry Idea

Dried fruits are a good lowfat source of energy. They can also contribute iron to your diet and sweeten foods without the addition of refined sugar. A bit of dried fruit compote is a tasty addition to hot cereals such as oatmeal.

DRIED FRUIT COMPOTE WITH GINGER AND LIME

4 SERVINGS

12 ounces (about ¾ cup) mixed dried fruit
(apricots, pitted prunes, and dried cherries are nice)
3 slices fresh ginger
1 lime, thinly sliced
1½ cups water
1½ cups apple juice
3 allspice berries (whole allspice)
2 tablespoons toasted pine nuts for garnish

Toss the fruit in a medium saucepan, then add the ginger, lime, water, juice, and allspice berries. Bring to a boil over medium heat, then reduce the heat to low. Cover loosely and simmer gently until the fruit is tender, about 45 minutes. Remove the allspice berries and discard. Serve compote warm, sprinkled with the pine nuts. The compote will keep, refrigerated, for about 2 weeks.

Note: To toast pine nuts without added fat, toss them into a dry nonstick sauté pan. Heat on medium-high and stir frequently until the nuts are toasted, about 1½ to 2 minutes.

Be a Fiber Finder

Barley and oat bran contain both forms of fiber — the insoluble kind that promotes digestive health and the soluble fiber that helps lower cholesterol levels. Barley, best known for its role in soups and side dishes, makes a delicious and hearty breakfast.

BARLEY BREAKFAST PUDDING WITH PECANS

4 SERVINGS

2 cups cooked barley
¼ cup maple syrup
⅓ cup pear or apple juice
1 pear or apple, cored and medium-chopped
¼ cup finely chopped dried dates
¼ teaspoon freshly grated nutmeg
¼ teaspoon cinnamon
⅓ cup chopped pecans
lowfat vanilla yogurt for serving

Preheat the oven to 350°F.

Spray a 2-quart casserole dish with nonstick vegetable spray. Then toss in the barley, maple syrup, juice, pear or apple, dates, nutmeg, cinnamon, and pecans. Stir well to combine.

Cover and bake until cooked through and fragrant, about 25 minutes. Serve warm topped with vanilla yogurt.

Fiber in Your Future

Adding cracked wheat, wheat germ, and wheat bran to yeast breads will increase their fiber and nutrient content. About a handful per loaf, added to the dough, works well and won't leave a gummy texture.

CRACKED WHEAT CINNAMON AND RAISIN BREAD

MAKES 1 LOAF

This bread freezes well and makes great toast.

½ cup medium-cracked wheat
2 cups warm water (110°F.)
3 tablespoons canola or safflower oil
1 tablespoon sugar
1 package active dry yeast
10 ounces (about 2 cups) unbleached white flour, unsifted
8 ounces (about 2 cups) unsifted whole wheat bread flour
extra flour for kneading
½ teaspoon salt
1½ teaspoon cinnamon
½ cup raisins

In a medium bowl combine the cracked wheat, water, oil, sugar, and yeast. Stir a bit so the yeast dissolves, then let sit for about 10 minutes, or until the wheat is fairly soft.

Meanwhile, in a large bowl combine the flours, salt, cinnamon, and raisins. When the cracked wheat is ready, add the flour mixture to it and stir to form a dough. Toward the end of mixing, it's easiest to use your hands.

Tip the dough out onto a floured counter and knead for about 8 minutes, kneading in extra flour if necessary. Set the dough into a bowl that's been sprayed with nonstick vegetable spray and turn the dough so all sides are moist. Cover the bowl with plastic wrap and let the dough rise until doubled in size, about 45 to 60 minutes.

Punch the dough down with your fist, then form it into a loaf. Set the loaf into a metal 9 x 5-inch loaf pan that's been sprayed with nonstick vegetable spray. Cover loosely with plastic wrap and let rise again for about 30 minutes. Preheat the oven to 350°F.

When the loaf is ready, spray the top with water from a plant mister, then bake on the center oven rack until the bottom sounds hollow when thumped, about 55 minutes.

If you're in the mood to fuss, after about 40 minutes of baking, remove the bread from the pan and let it continue to bake directly on the rack in the oven. Let the bread cool on a wire rack on the counter before slicing.

Flash in the Pan

If you use glass or black baking pans instead of stainless steel for your whole-grain breads, reduce the baking time by 5 to 10 minutes, or lower the oven temperature by about 25 degrees. If you don't, the outsides may bake before the insides are done.

LEMON-ZUCCHINI QUICK BREAD

MAKES 1 LOAF

1/3 cup maple syrup
1/3 cup canola or safflower oil
2 eggs, beaten
1 teaspoon vanilla extract
1 cup grated, drained zucchini
3 ounces (about 2/3 cup) unbleached flour
2½ ounces (about 2/3 cup) whole wheat pastry flour
2 teaspoons baking powder
¼ teasoon salt
1 teaspoon cinnamon
½ teaspoon freshly ground allspice
1 tablespoon finely grated lemon peel (yellow part only)
2/3 cup raisins

Preheat the oven to 375°F.

In a large bowl whisk together the maple syrup, oil, eggs, and vanilla. Be sure all ingredients are well combined, then stir in the zucchini.

In another large bowl sift together the flours, baking powder, salt, cinnamon, and allspice. Stir in the lemon zest and raisins.

Pour the wet ingredients into the dry flour mixture and use a large rubber spatula in broad strokes to combine well. Don't overmix. Spray an 8½ x 4½ x 2½-inch loaf pan with nonstick vegetable spray and scoop in the batter. Bake on center oven rack until the edges begin to brown and a thin knife comes out clean when inserted in the middle, about 50 to 55 minutes. Let cool on a wire rack before slicing.

Variation: To make muffins, pour the batter into paper-lined muffin tins; then bake until the tops are puffed and a knife comes out clean when inserted, about 18 to 20 minutes. For a special brunch treat, slice the muffins in half crosswise, then spread with lowfat cream cheese. Put the halves back together and serve in a bread basket lined with a pretty napkin.

PINTO BEAN BREAD

MAKES 1 LOAF

2½ ounces (about ½ cup) whole wheat bread flour
2 ounces (about ½ cup) unbleached flour
2 teaspoons baking powder
½ teaspoon baking soda
1 cup yellow cornmeal
1 tablespoon sugar
1¼ cups buttermilk
1 egg, lightly beaten
3 tablespoons canola or safflower oil
1 cup cooked pinto beans

Preheat the oven to 425°F.

In a large bowl sift together the flours, baking powder, baking soda, cornmeal, and sugar.

In a medium bowl combine the buttermilk, egg, and oil. Pour the liquid ingredients into the dry, add the beans, and stir until just combined. Don't overmix.

Spray an 8 x 8-inch pan with nonstick vegetable spray and scoop in the batter, smoothing the top with a spatula or your hand. Bake on center oven rack until the top is golden and a knife comes out clean when inserted, about 20 minutes. Let the bread cool in the pan on a wire rack for five minutes. Then cut into squares and serve.

Better Breads

Most bread recipes that call for only white flour can become higher in fiber and nutrients by replacing half the white flour with an equal amount of whole wheat flour. For yeast- and loaf-type breads, use whole wheat bread flour; for muffins and cake-type breads, use whole wheat pastry flour.

ORANGE MARMALADE BREAD

MAKES 1 LOAF

This bread makes great toast, but since it contains so little fat it won't stay fresh for longer than a day or two.

> *8 ounces (about 2 cups) whole wheat bread flour*
> *10 ounces (about 2 cups) unbleached flour*
> *½ teaspoon salt*
> *1 tablespoon baking powder*
> *½ cup orange marmalade, room temperature*
> *1½ cups buttermilk*
> *extra flour for shaping*

Preheat the oven to 425°F.

In a large bowl sift together the flours, salt, and baking powder. In a medium bowl whisk together the marmalade and buttermilk. Pour it into the dry ingredients and combine well. It's easiest to use your hands.

When the dough is almost combined, dump it out onto a floured counter and continue to combine while you shape it into a mound that's about 7 inches in diameter. Smooth out any cracks while you're shaping. Then line a cookie sheet with parchment paper and set the dough on it. Use a sharp knife to slash an "X" in the top, about ½-inch deep. This will keep the loaf from splitting while it rises. Sprinkle a bit of flour on the top of the loaf, then bake until the bottom of the loaf sounds hollow when you thump it, about 50 minutes.

Let bread cool on a wire rack about 20 minutes before slicing.

Wire Wisdom

 To avoid mushy bottoms on baked goods, let them cool on wire racks so that air can circulate around.

CHIVE AND CHEDDAR SCONCES

MAKES ABOUT 3 DOZEN

5 ounces (about 1 cup) unbleached flour
4 ounces (about 1 cup) whole wheat bread flour
1 teaspoon baking soda
2 teaspoons cream of tartar
¼ cup sweet butter or margarine, melted and slightly cooled
1 cup grated reduced-fat cheddar
¼ teaspoon dried dill weed
½ cup minced fresh chives
¾ cup buttermilk
extra flour for rolling

Preheat the oven to 425°F.

In a large bowl sift together the flours, baking soda, and cream of tartar. Then add the butter, cheddar, dill, chives, and buttermilk and mix with a large spatula.

Roll the dough out on a floured counter until it's about ¼-inch thick. Cut out 2½-inch rounds, placing them on a cookie sheet that's been sprayed with nonstick vegetable spray. (You may need 2 sheets.)

When all the scones are on the cookie sheet(s), dust them lightly with flour and bake until golden, about 8 to 10 minutes. Let cool on wire racks, then serve warm or room temperature.

Salt Smarts

Salt is needed in yeast breads for proper texture. The good news: All that's needed is ½ teaspoon per loaf, so adjust your favorite recipes accordingly.

Paper Pointer

In many recipes you can avoid the oil used to grease a bread pan if you line it with parchment paper instead.

GOLDEN ONION-DILL BREAD

MAKES 1 LOAF

6 ounces (about 1½ cups) whole wheat bread flour
6½ ounces (about 1½ cups) unbleached flour
½ cup wheat germ
2 packages active dry yeast
1 tablespoon sugar
1 tablespoon dried dill weed, or 3 tablespoons minced fresh
½ teaspoon salt
1 cup plain lowfat yogurt
½ cup water
2 tablespoons sweet butter or margarine
½ cup finely minced onion
2 egg whites

In a large bowl stir together two cups of the flour with the wheat germ, yeast, sugar, dill, and salt.

Combine the yogurt and water in a small saucepan and begin to simmer over medium heat. (The yogurt may break; that's ok.) Add the butter and onion and stir until the butter has melted. When the mixture is about 110°F. add it to the dry ingredients along with the egg whites. Use a hand mixer to beat at medium speed for about two minutes. Pour in the remaining flour, ¼ cup at a time, and stir until combined.

Line a 2-quart casserole dish with parchment paper, then scoop in the batter. Cover with plastic wrap and let rise until double in size, about 60 to 70 minutes.

Preheat the oven to 375°F. Bake the bread until golden, about 40 minutes. Let cool on a wire rack for ten minutes, then unmold and slice.

RYE AND CARAWAY FLATBREAD

MAKES 18 LARGE CRACKERS

Delicious with mild white cheese or as an accompaniment to soups and salads. Store in tightly covered containers.

4½ ounces (about 1 cup) rye flour
4 ounces (about 1 cup) whole wheat pastry flour
½ teaspoon salt
¼ cup sweet butter or margarine, melted and slightly cooled
1 teaspoon caraway seeds
¼ to ⅓ cup water

Preheat the oven to 425°F.

Measure the flours and salt into a large bowl. Then pour in the butter and use a pastry blender to combine well, mixing in the seeds and water as you go. When you have a workable dough, you've added enough water.

Divide the dough in half and knead each half until smooth and pliable, about 2 minutes. Then roll each half into a 9-inch square. Use a knife to cut out 3-inch crackers, then use a fork to poke a few air holes in each.

Line a large cookie sheet with parchment paper and arrange the crackers on it. Bake on center oven rack until the crackers just begin to be burnished, about 12 minutes. Let cool on a wire rack, then serve.

The Bran Plan

For extra fiber in muffins, replace about ¼ to ⅓ of the flour in a recipe with wheat or oat bran. Wheat bran is tasty and goes well with bold, molasses-type flavors; oat bran is good with fruity, more delicate recipes.

CARROT BRAN MUFFINS

MAKES 1 DOZEN

3 ounces (about 1 cup) wheat bran
1 cup buttermilk
6 ounces (about 1½ cups) whole wheat pastry flour
2 teaspoons baking powder
½ cup (about 3 medium) grated carrots
½ cup dried currants
1 egg, beaten
2 tablespoons canola or other vegetable oil
⅓ cup Barbados molasses
1½ teaspoons vanilla extract

Preheat the oven to 400°F.

Soak the bran in the buttermilk for about 10 minutes. Meanwhile, in a large bowl, sift together the flour and baking powder. Then add the carrot and currants and toss to combine well.

In a small bowl whisk together the egg, oil, molasses, and vanilla.

Add the bran mixture to the flour, then scoop in the egg mixture. Use a large spatula and large strokes to combine the batter — about 12 to 15 strokes will do. Don't overmix.

Line muffin tins with paper liners and scoop in the batter, filling cups equally. Bake until cooked through, about 20 minutes. Let cool on a wire rack before enjoying.

No Fat Needed

Instead of pouring on the oil, use paper liners to line muffin tins. The muffins won't stick, and you'll cut down on fat and calories.

EVER-READY MUFFINS

MAKES 1 DOZEN

7 ounces (about 1¾ cups) whole wheat pastry flour
3½ ounces (about ¾ cup) unbleached flour
1 teaspoon baking powder
1 teaspoon baking soda
1 tablespoon instant nonfat dry milk
3 tablespoons canola or other vegetable oil
¼ cup honey
¼ cup Barbados molasses
1½ cups buttermilk

In a large bowl, sift together the flours, baking powder, baking soda, and dry milk.

In a medium bowl whisk together the oil, honey, molasses, and buttermilk. Scoop into the flour mixture and use a large spatula to combine well. Don't overmix—about 12 to 15 strokes will do.

Here's the ever-ready part: Scoop the batter into a container, seal tightly and refrigerate. The batter will keep for about 3 weeks.

When you're ready, bake a dozen or just 1 or 2. Preheat the oven to 400°F, line the muffin tins with paper liners, scoop in the batter, and bake for about 18 minutes. If you're baking less than a dozen muffins, pour a bit of water into each of the unfilled muffin tins.

Muffins in a Minute

If your mornings are hectic, here's how to have a quick and healthful breakfast: Bake a batch of muffins, seal in a plastic bag and freeze. When you're ready, wrap 2 muffins in a damp paper towel and microwave on full power until warm and tender, about 1 minute. Let stand for about 30 seconds, then devour. Or wrap in a napkin and take them with you.

Make-Ahead Muffins

Measure and combine the dry ingredients for muffins in advance. Wet ingredients can also be prepared ahead and refrigerated. Then, when you're ready, preheat the oven, combine the ingredients, and bake. This is a convenient way to have a freshly baked, high-fiber treat in a hurry.

OAT MUFFINS WITH APRICOTS AND PECANS

MAKES 1 DOZEN

4 ounces (about 1 cup), unsifted whole wheat pastry flour
6 ounces (about 2 cups) quick oats
½ teaspoon salt
¼ cup sugar
½ cup chopped dried apricots
½ cup chopped pecans
1 cup buttermilk
1 egg, beaten
¼ cup canola or other vegetable oil

Preheat the oven to 400°F.

In a large bowl combine the flour, oats, salt, sugar, apricots, and pecans.

In a medium bowl whisk together the buttermilk, egg, and oil. Pour into the dry ingredients and use a large spatula to combine well. Don't overmix — about 12 to 15 strokes will do.

Line muffin tins with paper liners and scoop in the batter. Bake until lightly browned and cooked through, about 18 minutes. Let cool on a wire rack before serving.

Get Fresh

Fresh fruit spreads are a great low-calorie, lowfat alternative to butter.

RASPBERRY PRESERVES

MAKES ABOUT 2 CUPS

This spread is delicious on toast, muffins, pancakes, and waffles. It will keep for about a month if refrigerated.

4 cups (approximately 2 pints) raspberries
   (black, red, or a mixture of both)
½ cup white grape juice
½ cup apple juice
juice and pulp of 1 lemon
⅓ cup sugar

Wash berries, remove stems, and dry well on paper towels. Tip the berries into a deep, 12-inch fry pan and mash them coarsely with a spatula. Add the juices, lemon, and sugar and bring to a boil. Continue to boil, stirring frequently, until thick and syrupy, about 15 minutes. Let cool and store in the refrigerator in a tightly closed jar.

Fruitful Fiber

Eating a piece of fruit may be a better health move than downing a glass of juice. Not that you shouldn't drink juice, but a whole orange has more fiber than the equivalent amount of orange juice and research shows that you feel fuller after eating a whole fruit than after quaffing down its juice.

Blender Breakfasts

If your life is busy—and even if it's not—you can create easy, lowfat drinkable breakfasts in your blender. Use fresh fruit, juices, lowfat dairy products—and your imagination.

ORANGE-BANANA BUTTERMILK

1 SERVING

½ cup cold orange juice
1 banana, peeled and quartered
½ cup cold buttermilk
¼ cup cold lowfat vanilla yogurt

Combine all of the ingredients in a blender and whiz until thick and smooth.

PINEAPPLE-MELON BREAKFAST SHAKE

1 SERVING

½ cup cold plain lowfat yogurt
½ cup chopped ripe cantaloupe
½ cup chopped ripe pineapple
2 ice cubes

Combine all of the ingredients in a blender and whiz until thick and smooth.

THREE-FRUIT COOLER

1 SERVING

½ cup cold purple grape juice
½ cup cold orange juice
1 banana, peeled and quartered

Combine all of the ingredients in a blender and whiz until thick and smooth.

BERRY BLENDER BREAKFAST

1 SERVING

1 cup fresh raspberries
½ cup cold plain lowfat yogurt
½ teaspoon vanilla
1 teaspoon sugar if the raspberries aren't sweet

Combine all of the ingredients in a blender and whiz until thick and smooth.

BANANA-MOCHA SHAKE

1 SERVING

1 banana, peeled and quartered
½ cup cold skim milk
½ cup cold lowfat vanilla yogurt
½ teaspoon instant coffee
1 teaspoon sugar

Combine all of the ingredients in a blender and whiz until thick and smooth.

Super Soups and Stews

Soups may have a hearty, homey image, but many of them deserve to be thought of as healthful and slimming. For one thing, a nutrient-dense liquid is usually lower in fat and calories than solid food. For another, soups can keep us from overeating, especially if they're hot, because we'll eat slower and be aware as soon as we're full.

Salt-Free Savor

The two culprits that prevent most soups from being healthful are fat and salt. You may know ways to cut fat from soups, and we'll show you more. But reducing salt while keeping flavors interesting is a bigger challenge. And to be successful, we must take a look at the tongue.

There may be more going on in your mouth than you know. To begin with, taste buds can only preceive four tastes — sweet, salty, sour, and bitter. (Flavors like "nutty," "fruity," and "earthy" are interpreted by our sense of smell. And "piquant," which we sense in hot peppers, is an actual chemical reaction that occurs in the mouth.) The sweet taste buds are at the tip of the tongue. Those that detect salt are just behind them and those that account for sour and bitter are in the back.

What all this means is that when we reduce salt we can stimulate the remaining three tastes in order to create a full flavor in the mouth. Then soup—and other foods—won't taste bland. Let's say we're taking the salt out of a chicken-vegetable soup. We'll add a little sweet, maybe a carrot or sweet potato; then a little sour, like white wine; and for the bitter, a pinch of fresh lemon zest. Suddenly, these taste buds become excited, responses are sent to the brain, and we taste something that's delicious and interesting—without salt.

Now let's advance to what's called "bloom." The best way to describe it is to say that the whole mouth seems to light up with tastes. It happens with certain wines and can also happen in reduced-salt soups by adding aromatics. These are foods that *smell* good, like garlic, leeks, herbs, ginger, and citrus. So let's go back to our chicken-vegetable soup and make it bloom. If you're thinking of adding garlic and leeks, you'd be making a good choice. Onion and scallion would be nice, too.

An equally important taste tip for reduced-salt soups is to be aware of temperature. Cold numbs the tongue so that the taste buds perceive less. Have you ever noticed that melted ice cream seems to taste sweeter than it does when it's frozen? Temperature is the reason. So hot, warm, and room temperature soups will seem more flavorful than chilled ones, especially without salt. If you're serving a chilled soup, add aromatics to taste and refrigerate overnight to allow time for the flavors to mingle.

The recipes in this chapter were created with all of this in mind. Read through and discover all the secrets. Then you'll be able to convert almost any soup recipe to be a healthful and delicious one.

Taking Stock

The best way to guarantee nutritious, delicious soups is to start with a great stock. We recommend you make your own so you'll know exactly what's in it. This requires just a small amount of time on your part. Best of all, stocks store well, so you can make a lot and freeze some for later.

The basic stock formula is:

- 2 pounds of bones
- About 3½ cups of vegetables and aromatics
- About 6 cups of cold water.

Put all the ingredients in a large, heavy-bottomed pot and simmer on very low heat, loosely covered. Cooking time will vary, depending on the type of stock you're making, so check the chart. Strain the stock, then cool it quickly in a sink of ice water. This will give you the purest flavor. Next, set the stock in the refrigerator overnight. When next you see it, the fat will have come to the top and hardened and can be removed by lifting it off with a spatula. Then use or freeze the stock for up to 12 months. Yield will be about 1¼ quarts.

You'll use your stocks to create soups, of course, but remember, too, that they also make wonderful lowfat, low-salt and low-calorie additions to sauces and wherever liquid is needed in a recipe.

Stocking Up

Stock	Bones	Vegetables and Aromatics	Water	Time	Notes
Chicken	2 pounds	onion, leek, carrot, celery, parsley, bay leaf	6 cups	2 hours	
Turkey	2 pounds	onion, carrot, celery, sage, peppercorns	6 cups	2 hours	
Beef	2 pounds	onion, carrot, celery, tomato, thyme, bay leaf, peppercorns, whole cloves	6 cups	3–4 hours	Brown bones under broiler first
Fish	2 pounds	leek, carrot, celery, bay leaf, fennel	6 cups	½ hour	Use bones or heads
Vegetable	—	spinach, tomato, leek, parsnip, dried mushrooms, bay leaf, thyme	6 cups	½ hour	

Beef It Up

One great thing to do with beef stock is make *demi-glace* (DEM-ee–GLAZE). This is a concentrate of beef stock that adds flavor — without fat — to soups and sauces.

DEMI-GLACE

MAKES ABOUT 1½ CUPS

The flavor of demi-glace is robust, so you'll never need to salt. Use about 1 teaspoon or to taste for each 2 cups of liquid in soups, 1½ teaspoons to 1 cup of sauce.

1¼ quarts beef stock
½ cup dry red wine

Pour beef stock into a large heavy-bottomed soup pot. Add red wine and bring to a boil. Reduce the heat to a very low simmer and continue to simmer, uncovered, until the stock has reduced to about 1½ cups, about 2 hours. Stir occasionally and take care the glace doesn't burn.

Let it cool, then store refrigerated for about a month, or frozen for about 6 months.

Clever with Calcium

While making stock, help release the calcium from the bones by adding a small amount of acid. Tomato, lemon juice, or vinegar will do the trick.

Three Ideas for Quick Lowfat Soups

- Add couscous and minced fresh mint to boiling chicken stock. Cover, remove from heat and let stand until the couscous is tender, about 5 minutes. Serve warm.
- Simmer skinny Chinese noodles in chicken stock. Garnish with minced scallion and toasted sesame seeds and serve warm.
- Add chopped tomato, minced leek, and a pinch of basil to hot beef stock. Serve warm with garlic bread on the side.

AVOCADO-CUCUMBER SOUP

4 SERVINGS

1 cucumber, peeled, seeded and cubed
1 ripe avocado, peeled, pitted, and cubed
2 scallions, minced
2 tablespoons freshly squeezed lemon juice
2 cups plain lowfat yogurt
½ cup chicken stock
¼ teaspoon hot pepper sauce, or to taste
2 tablespoons fresh parsley

Combine all of the ingredients in a processor or blender and whiz until smooth. Serve at room temperature or very slightly chilled.

Out of Stock

If you run out of homemade stock, a fair alternative is reduced-salt bouillon granules. Keep a jar on hand to use when you need it. And further reduce salt by starting with less than the recommended amount. If you need more, you can always add it.

SPRING VEGETABLE SOUP

4 SERVINGS

1 tablespoon olive oil
2 medium leeks, cleaned and chopped
3 cups chicken stock
2 cups spinach, washed well and chopped
2 cups watercress, washed and chopped
4 scallions, minced
1 cup milk

Warm a large soup pot over medium heat, then pour in the oil. Add the leeks and sauté until they're tender, about 7 minutes.

Pour in the chicken stock and bring to a boil. Then reduce the heat to medium, toss in the spinach, watercress, and scallions and simmer until the greens are just wilted, about 5 minutes.

Let the soup "relax" for about 5 minutes, then pour into a processor or blender (in batches if necessary), add the milk and whiz until smooth but still flecked with green. Serve warm or at room temperature.

FRESH TOMATO SOUP WITH LEEKS

4 SERVINGS

1 tablespoon olive oil
1 medium leek, cleaned well and finely chopped
4 rich, ripe tomatoes, peeled, seeded, and chopped
1½ cups chicken stock
1½ cups beef stock
1 tablespoon very finely minced fresh dill, or ½ teaspoon dried

Warm a large soup pot over medium heat, then add the olive oil. Add the leek and sauté until tender, about 7 minutes.

Add the tomatoes and sauté for about a minute more. Pour in the stocks, bring the soup to a boil, then reduce the heat and simmer until heated through and fragrant, about 5 minutes. Stir in the dill and serve hot.

Zap That Fat

To remove drops of fat from a soup, set a large lettuce leaf on top. Let it float there for about 2 minutes, then remove and discard, fat and all.

EGGPLANT SOUP WITH TINY WHITE BEANS

4 SERVINGS

1 tablespoon olive oil
1 medium onion, minced
2 cloves garlic, peeled and minced
¼ cup minced fresh celery leaves
2 cups cubed eggplant, unpeeled
6 Italian plum tomatoes, peeled and seeded (or canned)
2 cups chicken stock
¼ teaspoon thyme
¼ teaspoon rosemary
1 cup cooked tiny white beans
  (if you use canned, rinse them first)
2 tablespoons freshly grated parmesan for sprinkling

Warm a large soup pot over medium heat, then add the olive oil. When it's warm, add the onion, garlic, and celery leaves; sauté until fragrant and just wilted, about 3 minutes.

Add the eggplant and tomatoes, cover and let the vegetables simmer for about 7 minutes. Stir in the stock, thyme, and rosemary and continue to simmer until the eggplant is tender, about 20 minutes. Add the beans, heat through and serve hot, sprinkled with the parmesan.

Hooray for Purees

 Pureeing soups in a processor or blender will make them thick and creamy without the addition of fatty cream or egg yolks.

ZUCCHINI PUREE WITH TOASTED CUMIN

4 SERVINGS

8 ripe medium tomatoes, quartered
1 sweet red pepper, seeded and quartered
1 stalk celery, including leaves, chopped
½ sweet onion, chopped
juice and pulp of 1 lemon
¼ cup chopped fresh basil or 1 teaspoon dried
½ teaspoon grated lemon zest (yellow part only)
2 small zucchini, chopped
2 teaspoons cumin seed

Combine the tomatoes, pepper, celery, onion, lemon juice, basil, lemon zest, and zucchini in a processor or blender and whiz until smooth. (Be patient, this could take a couple of minutes.)

Refrigerate the soup for at least 3 hours (or even overnight) to give the flavors time to mingle.

Meanwhile, to toast the cumin, toss the seeds into a dry non-stick pan over medium-high heat. Stir frequently. Then crush in a mortar. Serve the soup very slightly chilled or at room temperature sprinkled with the cumin.

Variation: If you prefer, substitute fennel seed or dill seed for the cumin.

The Grain Gain

Adding grains such as rice, barley, and buckwheat to soups puts lowfat fiber into your diet. Beans and other legumes will do the same.

FRESH VEGETABLE SOUP WITH WILD RICE

4 SERVINGS

1 tablespoon olive oil
1 medium onion, chopped
1 leek, chopped
2 carrots, finely chopped
1 stalk celery, with leaves, finely chopped
large handful green beans (about 4 ounces),
    ends and strings removed
¼ pound winter squash, peeled and chopped
    (butternut is best)
2 bay leaves
3 cloves garlic, mashed through a press
4 cups chicken stock
¼ cup wild rice, uncooked
½ teaspoon thyme
½ teaspoon basil

Warm a large soup pot over medium heat. Add the oil; when it's hot, add the onion, leek, carrots, celery, beans, squash, bay leaves, and garlic. Sauté until the vegetables are fragrant and just wilted, about 10 minutes.

Pour in the stock and rice and bring to a boil. Reduce the heat to a simmer and continue to simmer, loosely covered, for about an hour, stopping midway to add the thyme and basil. Serve hot.

Shake the Salt

Instead of using salt in soups, make the flavors bloom with wine. Dry whites are good with lighter soups and those with a chicken stock base. Dry reds harmonize with soups with a beef stock base. If the recipe calls for 4 cups of stock, use 3½ instead plus ½ cup of wine.

Roux How-To

Many soups, stews, and sauces are based on what's called a "roux" (roo). This is a paste of flour and fat that imparts color, flavor, and texture wherever it's added. The resulting sauce can be horribly high in fat and calories, however. Fortunately, our Healthful Roux below shows you how to create a no-fat-added, low-calorie roux that's even better than the traditional version.

Scoop ⅓ cup unbleached flour into a dry nonstick sauté pan and heat on high, stirring constantly with a wooden spatula, to toast the flour and bring out a rich, roasted flavor. This will take about 7 minutes, so be patient; keep stirring and don't let the flour burn. When the flour is fragrant and medium-light brown, remove the pan from the heat and whisk in ⅔ cup room-temperature stock. Continue to whisk until smooth.

Now the roux is ready to enhance soup for four or, in small amounts, to spike sauces. You can also cover and refrigerate the roux for up to a week later.

CHICKEN GUMBO

4 SERVINGS

⅓ cup unbleached flour
⅔ cup room temperature beef stock
1 sweet red pepper, cored, seeded, and finely chopped
1 green pepper, cored, seeded, and finely chopped
1 stick celery, with leaves, finely chopped
1 onion, finely chopped
2 scallions, finely chopped
1 teaspoon thyme
½ teaspoon hot pepper sauce, or to taste
3½ cups beef stock
½ pound boneless, skinless chicken cutlet, coarsely chopped
¼ pound okra, cut to 1-inch pieces
cooked rice for serving

Pour the flour into a large nonstick sauté pan and heat on high. Stir the flour frequently with a wooden spatula and continue to heat until the flour is toasted — about 7 minutes. Remove from the heat and pour in the ⅔ cup of stock, whisking well to combine. Immediately add the red and green peppers, celery, onion, scallions, thyme and hot pepper sauce and stir to combine. Continue with the gumbo or refrigerate the roux until you need it, up to a week.

Bring the beef stock to a boil in a large soup pot, then add the roux and chicken, stirring well to combine. Reduce the heat and let the gumbo simmer, loosely covered, until slightly thickened, about 20 minutes.

Meanwhile, heat a nonstick sauté pan over medium heat; toss in the okra. Let the okra cook, stirring frequently, until just tender, about 7 to 10 minutes. Add it to the gumbo and serve hot in shallow bowls over little mounds of rice.

Variation: Substitute green beans for the okra, adding them to the gumbo when you add the chicken.

Soup in a Snap

Freeze individual portions of homemade soup in wide, flat plastic or glass containers. When you're ready for a wholesome meal or snack, microwave on medium power until defrosted.

SAVORY COD STEW

4 SERVINGS

1 tablespoon olive oil
1 medium onion, chopped
1 stalk celery, with leaves, chopped
2 cloves garlic, mashed through a press
1 sweet red pepper, cored, seeded and coarsely chopped
1 bay leaf
1 teaspoon oregano
1 teaspoon basil
¼ cup fish or chicken stock
¼ cup dry white wine
1 sprig parsley
2 medium tomatoes, seeded and chopped
½ teaspoon hot pepper sauce, or to taste
1 pound cod fillet, cut into 1-inch pieces

Warm a large soup pot over medium heat and pour in the oil. When the oil is warm toss in the onion, celery, garlic, red pepper, and bay leaf. Sauté until the vegetables are fragrant and slightly tender, about 5 to 6 minutes.

Add the oregano, basil, stock, wine, parsley, tomatoes, and hot pepper sauce and bring to a boil. Reduce the heat, cover loosely and simmer for about 10 minutes. Gently slip in the cod and continue to simmer until cooked through, about 5 minutes. Serve hot in shallow bowls with crusty bread for dunking.

FRAGRANT SHRIMP SOUP WITH GARLIC AND GINGER

---
4 SERVINGS

3 cups chicken or fish stock
¼ cup dry sherry
4 slices fresh ginger
3 cloves garlic, peeled and halved
1 pound medium shrimp, peeled and deveined
⅓ cup sliced wild or tame mushrooms
3 scallions, julienned

Pour the stock and sherry into a medium saucepan and add the ginger and garlic. Bring to a boil, then reduce the heat to a simmer. Continue to simmer, covered loosely, for about 5 minutes.

Use a slotted spoon to remove the ginger and garlic, then add the shrimp and mushrooms. Continue simmering, loosely covered, until the shrimp are pink and cooked through, about 5 minutes. Sprinkle on the scallions and serve warm.

Value-Added Soup

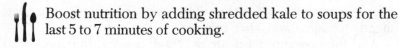 Boost nutrition by adding shredded kale to soups for the last 5 to 7 minutes of cooking.

Smooth as Silk

For the smoothest purees without added fat, press the food to be pureed through a sieve. It takes a bit of time but the texture is so silky, it's worth it.

LENTIL PUREE WITH ROASTED CHICKEN

4 SERVINGS

1 tablespoon olive oil
1 small onion, chopped
1 leek, cleaned and chopped
1 stalk celery, with leaves, chopped
1 carrot, chopped
1 clove garlic, mashed through a press
1 bay leaf
1 teaspoon thyme
1¼ cups lentils (soak first)
3½ cups to 4½ cups chicken stock
½ cup shredded kale
1 whole roasted chicken breast, cooked

Warm a large soup pot over medium heat and pour in the olive oil. When the oil is hot, tip in the onion, leek, celery, carrot, and garlic and sauté until fragrant and slightly wilted, about 7 minutes.

Toss in the bay leaf, thyme, lentils, and about 3 cups of stock and bring to a boil. Reduce heat, cover loosely and simmer until the lentils are tender, about 45 to 50 minutes. About 5 minutes before cooking time is up, add the kale.

Set a large strainer atop a large bowl and scoop in a bit of soup. Press soup through with the back of a large spoon and continue to scoop and press until all the soup has been sieved.

Put the soup back into the pot and begin to warm it slowly. If it's too thick, add a bit more stock. Meanwhile, skin the chicken and shred the meat into bite-sized pieces with your fingers. Add to the soup, heat through, and serve.

The Eyes Have It

Before food ever reaches our mouths, we form an opinion of it with our eyes. If it looks rich, we might think it tastes rich, even if it's not. Saffron colors food with rich golden hues, without a speck of fat, and is especially alluring in soups.

TURKEY SOUP WITH SAFFRON AND RICE

4 SERVINGS

1 tablespoon olive oil
1 leek, cleaned and finely chopped
1 carrot, finely chopped
3 cloves garlic, peeled and sliced
3 cups chicken stock
2 tomatoes, chopped
1 bay leaf
½ teaspoon saffron threads
1 cup cooked medium-grain brown rice
½ cup shredded cooked turkey
2 tablespoons minced fresh chives

Warm a large soup pot on medium heat. Pour in the olive oil, and when it's heated through toss in the leek, carrot, and garlic; sauté until fragrant and slightly wilted, about 5 minutes.

Pour in the stock, then add the tomatoes and bay leaf. Crush the saffron between your fingers and add to the soup. Bring the soup to a boil, reduce heat and simmer, loosely covered, for about 15 minutes.

Stir in the rice, turkey, and chives and heat through. Serve hot.

PASTA SOUP WITH PESTO

4 SERVINGS

4 cups chicken stock
1 cup orzo or other tiny pasta
2 cloves garlic, peeled and coarsely chopped
⅓ cup fresh basil
5 shelled pecans
2 teaspoons freshly grated parmesan
2 teaspoons olive oil
1 ripe Italian plum tomato, seeded and coarsely chopped

Pour the stock into a large soup pot and bring it to a boil. Add the orzo and continue to boil until tender, about 5 minutes.

Meanwhile, to make the pesto, combine the garlic, basil, pecans, parmesan, olive oil, and tomato in a processor or blender and whiz until you have a paste.

To serve, pour the hot soup into large bowls and scoop an equal amount of pesto into each.

A New Leaf

Fresh celery leaf has a robust flavor that will help you forget all about salt. Mince and use about 1 teaspoon per serving of soup. Don't overdo celery, however, if you're on a super-strict low-sodium diet.

Slim Surprise

Many people have switched from whole-milk dairy products to lowfat. One advantage is that on the rare occasion that they have whole milk, it tastes like heavy cream!

CORN AND PUMPKIN CHOWDER

4 SERVINGS

1 tablespoon olive oil
1 leek, cleaned and minced
½ pound neck pumpkin (not jack-o-lantern type),
*   peeled and diced*
1 medium potato (with or without peel), diced
1½ cups corn kernels
1 tablespoon minced celery leaf
1 teaspoon thyme
2 cups beef stock
2 cups milk (skim or whole)

Heat a large soup pot over medium heat, then add the olive oil. When it's hot, add the leek and sauté until fragrant and slightly wilted, about 5 minutes.

Add the pumpkin, potato, corn, celery, thyme, and stock and bring to a boil. Reduce the heat, cover loosely, and simmer until the vegetables are tender, about 15 to 20 minutes.

Pour in the milk and simmer gently until heated through. Serve warm.

Salads
and Sandwiches

At first, this chapter appears to be ideas for the perfect light lunch. And you'd be right to think so. Crisp greens with a light vinaigrette, jewels of marinated vegetables, and luscious yet lean sandwich fillings on interesting whole-grain breads definitely say "lunch." But we hope to encourage you to integrate these light foods into other meals as well.

Offer an enticing salad—such as Coral, Jade, and Ivory—as a first course with grilled chicken. Serve refreshing Avocado and Tangerine with Mustard Vinaigrette after poached fish instead of dessert. Create a brunch buffet composed of several salads surrounded by harmonious dressings, and let each person choose and toss his own. And as for daily dinner with the family, begin to think of salad as equal in importance to the entrée, not overshadowed by huge hunks of meat.

But no matter how low in calories, low in fat, and healthful these salads are, no one's going to eat them unless they're delicious. And recipes are only as good as the ingredients that go in them. So it's up to you to choose the best produce and store it well. When selecting greens, look for tender leaves that are a lively color for the particular variety. Avoid brown spots, soft spots, and dark, limp edges Store greens, unwashed, in perforated plastic bags in the crisper drawer of the refrigerator for up to a week.

Once you're ready to create a salad, combine greens that are compatible in taste and texture. Red leaf lettuce and spinach leaves are a pleasant combination, while winter cabbage and watercress make no sense together. Then pair the greens with the freshest produce of the season. Thinly sliced or chopped finely, these vegetables and fruits will release more flavor, without the addition of oil.

Next, choose a dressing that complements your salad. For example, spicy Chinese dressing would be great with tender greens, scallions, and a toss of cashews, but a complete disaster with fruit. And don't drown salads with too much dressing. Not only will it add unneeded calories and fat, but it can hide the taste of the salad ingredients. We use a maximum of 1 tablespoon of dressing per serving as a guideline. Also, pour it on just before you're ready to eat to prevent wilting. With large paddles, toss the salad 30 times so that everything is well but lightly coated. Wilting can also be avoided if the dressing is refrigerated before tossing.

While you're waiting for the salad dressing to chill, build a beautiful sandwich or two. Begin with a bread from the first chapter or choose a whole-grain store-bought loaf.

Although bread is the typical foundation for many of our sandwiches, others use grain-based alternatives and some use no bread at all. A crisp taco shell filled with flavorful marinated vegetables, for instance, is a delicious and healthful sandwich that many people have never considered. Even better, try egg rolls, the most ancient of all sandwiches; we've devised a way to make them crisp without deep-frying. And for the lowest calorie sandwich of all, try our fillings wrapped in a lettuce leaf.

For variety try our Muffaletta, which is a round bread that's hollowed out and filled with vegetables and herbs. It's a meal in itself. Or consult our sandwich composition chart and learn to make a BLT without the fatty bacon as well as snazzy little sandwiches you can use as a first course or to adorn an appetizer tray.

We've built in another incentive to entice you to prepare these selections instead of reaching for salty, surgary, fatty, caloric snack foods that are low in fiber and nutrients: These salads and sandwiches are quick and easy to make. Try them and you'll see that eating well can be a snap.

Isn't It Time to Change Your Oil?

Tablespoon for tablespoon, flavored oils have the same fat and calorie content as common oils. Thanks to their richer flavor, however, you can use smaller amounts, thereby reducing fat and calories. Try walnut oil, hazelnut oil, toasted sesame oil, avocado oil, peanut oil, or olive oil. Buy them in small bottles and store in a cool, dark place. These oils contain mostly mono- and polyunsaturated fats, which are associated with better blood cholesterol levels and therefore may help prevent heart disease.

WALNUT VINAIGRETTE

4 SERVINGS

2 tablespoons French walnut oil
1½ tablespoons sherry vinegar, cider vinegar, or other
mild amber vinegar
¼ teaspoon dijon-style mustard

In a small bowl, whisk all the ingredients until smooth and well combined. If you have a small electric spice grinder, whiz the dressing in it and it will become very thick and creamy. Either way, chill slightly before tossing with salad for four.

Salad Ideas for Walnut Vinaigrette

Serve Walnut Vinaigrette with:

• Cooked barley, chunked steamed zucchini, and chopped sweet red pepper

- Shredded poached chicken and cherry tomatoes, garnished with a few toasted walnuts
- Thinly sliced wild or tame mushrooms and curly red lettuce leaves

Herb Blurb

Fresh herbs add flavor without fat to dressings and salads. As if that's not enough, they also let you cut back on salt without sacrificing taste. Most produce sections carry at least one or two fresh herbs, even in winter.

CREAMY FRENCH HERB DRESSING

4 SERVINGS

3 tablespoons fresh basil, stems removed
pinch freshly grated lemon zest (without white part)
2 tablespoons part-skim ricotta
2 tablespoons buttermilk or lowfat milk

In a food processor or blender, whiz the basil until minced. Then add in the zest, ricotta, and buttermilk and continue to whiz until well combined and smooth. Chill slightly before tossing with salad for four.

Variation: Substitute fresh sage or dill for the basil.

Salad Ideas
for Creamy Fresh Herb Dressing

Serve this terrific dressing with

- Chunked cucumber, chunked tomato, baby corn, and scallions

- Cooked pasta, steamed broccoli, and steamed shrimp
- Steamed baby new potatoes and finely minced chives

SPICY CHINESE DRESSING

4 SERVINGS

1 tablespoon peanut oil
splash hot pepper sauce or to taste
1 tablespoon rice vinegar or other mild white vinegar
1 teaspoon regular or reduced-sodium soy sauce
1 clove garlic, peeled and very finely minced
½ teaspoon very finely minced fresh ginger
1 teaspoon honey

Combine all of the ingredients in a processor or blender and whiz until well combined. Chill slightly before tossing with salad for four.

Salad Ideas for
Spicy Chinese Dressing

Spicy Chinese Dressing is great with:

- Spinach, romaine, blanched snow peas, and minced scallion
- Ribbons of cooked flank steak, chopped purple onion, and steamed green beans
- Cooked rice, shredded cooked chicken, grated tart apple, and a pinch of curry powder served on a bed of romaine and sprinkled with minced scallions

Savor the Flavor

Citrus zest makes dressings and salads bloom with flavor so that you can reduce or eliminate the salt. Use a special little zester tool, available at many supermarkets, to ensure that you remove only the flavorful colored part and not the puckery white pith.

ORANGE-CIDER DRESSING

4 SERVINGS

2 tablespoons cider vinegar
1 tablespoon olive oil
¼ teaspoon dijon-style mustard
¼ teaspoon finely minced orange zest

Combine all of the ingredients in a blender or processor and whiz until well combined. Chill slightly before tossing with salad for four.

Salad Ideas for
Orange-Cider Dressing

Try this zingy dressing with:

- Cooked tiny white beans, minced sweet red pepper, minced fresh mint, and minced scallions
- Blanched asparagus spears
- Tender Swiss chard, sliced sweet onion, and chunky home-made croutons

Low in Fat, High in Flavor

Herbed and other flavored vinegars add an alluring range of tastes to salads and dressings, without contributing fat and calories. Most supermarkets offer a selection, including dill or tarragon vinegar. Use them to spark up salads and marinades.

CREATE YOUR OWN HERBED VINEGAR

4 SERVINGS

2 cloves garlic, peeled and smashed
1 sprig rosemary
1 tablespoon currants or dark raisins
1½ cups cider vinegar

In a medium saucepan combine all of the ingredients. Heat on medium until just warm and fragrant, about 3½ minutes. Don't boil.

Let the vinegar cool, then pour everything into a glass jar. Cover and store in a cool, dark place for about 10 days. Then it's ready to use. Store refrigerated for up to 3 months.

Four Seasons of
Sensational Salads

Spring

Mesclun is a French term for a fresh mixture of tender spring greens. For a simple approach, try a toss of watercress, young spinach, and young romaine. For something more exotic, mix arugula, maché, and red oak lettuce. But whatever combination you choose, dress it lightly with a splash of olive oil and freshly squeezed lemon juice and enjoy at room temperature for best flavor.

Steam tiny new potatoes — the tinier the better — until tender. Then toss with blanched fresh peas and minced chives. Splash with tarragon vinegar and serve warm.

Mix a quick and healthful dressing of plain lowfat yogurt, minced dill, and minced shallot. Then toss with blanched green beans and carrot coins.

Spring nutrition note: For an interesting and nutritious green, don't overlook dandelion. It's available, bagged, in many supermarkets and like other dark greens is higher in vitamins and minerals than its paler cousins. Toss with curly red lettuce and radish slices and dress with red wine vinegar and a splash of olive oil.

Summer

Toss blanched sweet corn kernels, sliced sweet peppers, and broccoli florets with a splash each of cider vinegar, olive oil, and hot pepper sauce. Serve on petals of green leaf lettuce.

Separate slices of purple onion into rings and combine with ripe tomato slices. Drizzle on a bit of olive oil, and sprinkle with freshly ground black pepper and minced thyme. Serve with crusty bread.

Make a coleslaw by combining shredded cabbage and grated carrot. Dress with reduced-calorie mayonnaise and minced fresh parsley.

Summer nutrition note. For low caloric, lowfat flavor, add whole fresh herb leaves and edible flowers to salads. Basil and small sage leaves are tasty herbs to try. And as for flowers, nasturtium, pea, and squash blooms are delicious and colorful.

Autumn

Combine a dark green, such as curly kale, with cooked fava beans and currants. Dress with a splash each of orange juice, lemon juice, and olive oil.

Toss together chopped apple, chopped celery, and chopped cucumber. Dress with plain lowfat yogurt that's been spiked with mint.

Chunk and steam a winter squash, such as butternut. Then toss with plain lowfat yogurt and a bit of prepared mustard. Sprinkle with minced scallion before serving warm.

Autumn nutrition note: Greens like mustard, turnip, and beet are delicious and extra high in vitamin A. For best results, choose small, tender leaves, then toss into salads with other vegetables.

Winter

Toss together julienned raw beets, carrots, and tender parsnips. Marinate in cider vinegar, a splash of olive oil, and a pinch of dill. Serve on mounds of spinach leaves.

Combine chard, sliced mushrooms, crisp bean sprouts, and sunflower seeds. Dress with lemon juice and a splash of peanut oil.

Steam chunks of turnips until tender. Then toss with soy sauce (preferably reduced-sodium), a mild white vinegar (such as rice vinegar) and minced garlic. Garnish with toasted sesame seeds and minced scallion and serve warm.

Winter nutrition tip: Add extra fiber to winter salads by tossing in cooked beans. Many people cook the beans ahead and store them in the freezer. They'll last for up to a year and defrost quickly.

Salt Lovers Love Lovage

Lovage is a tall, easy-to-grow herb that can be minced and used in salads and dressings to create a full taste without salt. It can be bought at many summer markets and it freezes well. Lovage is also available dried, but the flavor is not as alluring. Use only the leaves; the stems are tough and less tasty.

Mustard Magic

One secret to smooth, lower-oil dressings is using mustard, whether dried or prepared. Its emulsifying action promotes a smooth, silky texture without the usual levels of fat.

CORAL, JADE, AND IVORY

4 SERVINGS

2 large carrots, sliced to coins
1/3 pound (about 5) Brussels sprouts, stems removed, sliced
1/3 pound (about 4) small parsnips, sliced to coins
3 cups boiling water
1 tablespoon olive oil
1 tablespoon balsamic vinegar or other robust vinegar
1/4 teaspoon prepared dijon-style mustard
pinch freshly grated nutmeg

Add the carrots, sprouts, and parsnips to the boiling water and blanch for about 2 minutes. Drain well and pat dry. (Treat the sprouts gently or they may fall apart.)

In a small bowl whisk together the oil, vinegar, mustard, and nutmeg. Toss with the vegetables and serve at room temperature.

When Is a Salad Like a Soup?

Just as with soups, many salads seem more flavorful when eaten at room temperature. This is especially true with marinated vegetable salads, where taste and textures become more distinct when served at room temperature. Take care with lettuce salads, however; these can become limp in no time at all when left at room temperature.

MINESTRONE SALAD

4 SERVINGS

¼ pound green beans, tips and strings removed
boiling water for blanching
1 carrot, julienned
1 zucchini, peeled and julienned
3 scallions, minced
½ cup cooked small white or red beans
3 ripe tomatoes, juiced and chopped
¼ cup minced fresh basil or 1 tablespoon dried basil
2 tablespoons minced fresh flat-leaf parsley
2 tablespoons red wine vinegar
1 tablespoon freshly squeezed lemon juice
1 tablespoon olive oil
freshly ground black pepper to taste
1 tablespoon freshly grated Romano cheese for sprinkling

Blanch the green beans by adding to boiling water for 1 minute; add the carrot and zucchini, and boil for 1 minute longer. Drain and rinse under cold water and pat dry on paper towels.

In a large serving bowl toss together the green beans, carrot, zucchini, scallions, beans, tomatoes, basil, and parsley.

In a small bowl whisk together the vinegar, lemon juice, olive oil, and pepper. Pour it over the vegetables and toss well to combine. Sprinkle with the Romano and serve at room temperature.

Focus on Fine Wine

Using dry white wine as the acid in a salad dressing will enable you to eliminate or reduce salt while keeping the taste lively.

Clever Combinations

Fruit makes green salads come alive with flavor, at a small price in calories and fat. Oranges and pears are nice with spinach, for instance; apples and grapes are great in turkey salad.

AVOCADO AND TANGERINE WITH MUSTARD VINAIGRETTE

4 SERVINGS

1 small to medium bunch of romaine or other lettuce
2 tangerines, peeled, segmented, and seeded
1 small avocado, peeled, pitted, and sliced
2 tablespoons very finely minced fresh chives
1 tablespoon fruity (rather than aromatic) olive oil
1 tablespoon dry white wine
¼ teaspoon prepared dijon-style mustard
¼ teaspoon prepared country-style coarse mustard
pinch dry mustard

Trim the romaine and tear into pieces with your hands. This will keep the ends from becoming dark. (Head lettuce should be sliced with a knife.) Toss into a salad bowl with the tangerines, avocado, and chives.

To make dressing, whisk together the oil, wine, and mustards, then let the mixture chill slightly. Pour over the salad and toss 30 times to combine.

HOMEMADE CROUTONS (SANS SALT)

4 SERVINGS

2 teaspoons olive oil
2 cloves garlic, peeled
¼ teaspoon thyme
2 slices whole-grain bread, cubed

Pour the oil into a nonstick pan and toss in the garlic. Heat on medium-high until the oil is hot and the garlic is fragrant, about 2 minutes. Don't let the garlic burn.

Remove the garlic from the oil and discard. Sprinkle the thyme and bread cubes into the oil. Sauté until the cubes have toasted on all sides, about 3 minutes. Serve with salads or soups.

(The croutons will keep in a tightly closed glass jar for a couple of days.)

Smashing Secret

Vegetables such as cucumber and eggplant are often soaked in a salt solution before preparation so that they will better absorb surrounding flavors. But if they're gently smashed before being combined with other ingredients, no salt solution is necessary, and the final flavors are wonderful.

MARINATED EGGPLANT

4 SERVINGS

1 medium (about 1 to 1¼ pound), unpeeled eggplant
boiling water to cover
1 sweet yellow pepper, cored, seeded, and chopped
1 sweet red pepper, cored, seeded, and chopped
1 green bell pepper, cored, seeded, and chopped
2 tablespoons very finely minced sweet onion
1 clove garlic, peeled and very finely minced
1 tablespoon minced fresh basil or 1 teaspoon dried
2 tablespoons freshly squeezed lemon juice
1 tablespoon olive oil
freshly ground black pepper to taste
1 tablespoon crumbled feta cheese or to taste, for sprinkling

Halve the eggplant, then boil until tender, about 15 minutes. When it's cool enough to handle, chop into 1-inch square pieces and smash them gently with the bottom of a sauté pan.

Scoop the smashed eggplant into a medium bowl and add the peppers, onion, garlic, and basil.

In a small bowl whisk together the lemon juice, olive oil, and black pepper. Pour it over the eggplant mixture; cover and let marinate for about an hour. Serve at room temperature on pretty plates, sprinkled with the feta.

Six Sensational Sandwich Compositions

- To make a healthful twist on the BLT, start with whole-grain toast spread lightly with reduced-calorie mayonnaise. Add slices of rich, ripe tomato and deep green lettuce. Then sauté sliced, stemmed fresh shiitake mushrooms in a nonstick pan until fragrant and just a bit soft. Add to the sandwich instead of bacon.
- Remake of a famous classic: Stem watercress and slice cucumbers thinly. Arrange on thin slices of multi-grain bread that's been spread with reduced-calorie dilled mayonnaise.
- Halve a crusty onion roll and spread with part-skim ricotta. Layer with thin slices of tomato and purple onion. Then cover, wrap in foil, and bake in a hot (400°F.) oven until warm, about 7 minutes.
- Make a lower cholesterol egg salad using reduced-cholesterol eggs, which are available at many supermarkets and are 25 to 30 percent lower in cholesterol than normal eggs. Use plain lowfat yogurt to bind the salad and flavor with minced fresh herbs.
- Create a unique crabmeat sandwich. Combine crabmeat with chopped fresh green beans, minced sweet onion, and a bit each of dry mustard and hot pepper sauce. Bind with plain, lowfat yogurt or reduced-calorie mayonnaise. Serve in whole wheat pitas.
- Make an unusual high-fiber sandwich by filling a lettuce-lined pita with a combination of cooked great northern beans that have been tossed with a bit of olive oil, white wine vinegar, minced garlic, and freshly ground black pepper to taste.

Lower-Cal Butter

If you must use butter on sandwiches, try whipped butter, which contains 60 calories per tablespoon. Unwhipped butter, by contrast, contains 100 calories per tablespoon.

Lighten Up

The time may come when you're face to face with a sandwich and nothing but mayonnaise will do. In that case, use the mayo, but hold the fat. It's easy if you use a reduced-calorie mayonnaise, available at supermarkets. Or, you can make an even lighter version yourself.

AMAZING MAYO

MAKES ABOUT ¾ CUP

10½ ounces (about ¾ cup) silky-type tofu
1 tablespoon dry white wine
1 tablespoon freshly squeezed lemon juice
½ teaspoon prepared dijon-style mustard
1 tablespoon canola or olive oil
pinch salt

Combine all of the ingredients in a blender or processor and whiz until smooth. Refrigerate overnight to allow the flavors to mingle. The mayo will keep, covered and refrigerated, for about 2 weeks.

Variations: Flavor the mayo with herbs and spices to add interest to sandwiches and salads. Curry powder, dill, tarragon, or ground cumin are tasty additions.

TUNA SALAD WITH APPLE AND CHEDDAR

MAKES 4 SERVINGS

1 can (6½ ounces) water-packed tuna
½ cup shredded fresh spinach
¼ cup shredded reduced-calorie cheddar cheese
1 small apple, cored and finely minced
2 tablespoons finely minced onion
¼ cup plain lowfat yogurt
2 tablespoons reduced-calorie mayonnaise

Drain the tuna, then toss in a medium bowl with the spinach, cheese, apple, and onion.

In a small bowl combine the yogurt and mayonnaise, scoop into the tuna and mix well. Serve on whole-grain toast, whole-grain crackers, or in whole wheat pitas lined with lettuce.

Lettuce Teach You How to Wrap

Instead of spreading sandwich fillings on bread, roll them in lettuce leaves. This cuts calories and is especially refreshing for a summer lunch. Make lettuce sandwiches with tuna salad, crab salad, egg salad, or a little mound of marinated vegetables.

Great Grate Cheese

When using cheese on sandwiches, grate or shred it rather than slicing. A smaller amount will go further and you'll be saving fat and calories.

MUFFALETTA

MAKES 4 ENTRÉE SERVINGS
OR 8 SNACK SERVINGS

1 10-inch round loaf of crusty bread
1 tablespoon olive oil
⅓ cup grated reduced-calorie mozzarella cheese
4 artichoke bottoms, chopped
2 roasted sweet peppers, chopped (see page 84)
1 teaspoon balsamic vinegar or other robust vinegar
½ teaspoon oregano
½ teaspoon basil
2 scallions, minced
2 tablespoons crumbled feta cheese

Preheat the oven to 500°F.

Use a bread knife to slice the top third off the loaf. Then use a fork to scrape the bread away from the crust on both sections. (Freeze and save the scraped bread for poultry stuffing.)

Paint the bottom and sides of the larger bread portion with olive oil; then sprinkle in the mozzarella, artichokes, peppers, vinegar, oregano, basil, scallions, and feta. Cover with the top.

Wrap the entire loaf in foil, shiny-side-out, and bake until the cheese has melted and the bread has become even crustier, about 15 minutes. Unwrap, slice into wedges, and serve warm.

TACO SHELL SANDWICHES

You'll be surprised at the wonderful sandwiches you can invent by using crisp taco shells instead of bread. They're easy and delicious—and a corn tortilla can be half the calories of a slice of bread. Buy taco shells at the supermarket, giving preference to a brand made with an unsaturated oil. If you can't find any, make your own, using soft corn tortillas.

Preheat the oven to 500°F. Then hang each soft corn tortilla over two oven rungs, so it makes a little taco shape. Bake until crisp, about 7 minutes. Then fill and enjoy.

Ideas for Filling Taco Shells

Line the shell with lettuce, then pack with one of the following:

- Cooked beans, grated reduced-calorie cheese, and chopped olives
- Chicken or crabmeat salad
- Sliced ripe tomato, reduced-calorie mozzarella, and minced fresh basil

Variation: Any of these tasty ideas can be stuffed into a whole wheat pita, too.

Body-Guard Veggies

Cabbage, and other members of the cruciferous family of vegetables, can help guard your body against certain types of cancer. To get more cabbage into your life, use it to line sandwiches instead of lettuce, and add it shredded to sandwich fillings.

(UNFRIED) EGG ROLLS

MAKES 4 SERVINGS

A wonderful brunch or summer meal when served with a light soup or salad.

> 1 cup shredded white cabbage
> 1/3 cup chopped snow peas
> 1/3 cup mung bean sprouts
> 1/4 cup chopped water chestnuts
> 1 teaspoon reduced-sodium soy sauce
> 1 clove garlic, mashed through a press
> 2 scallions, very finely minced
> 1 teaspoon peanut butter
> 4 egg roll skins
> 1 egg white
> 1 tablespoon peanut oil

Spray a large nonstick pan with nonstick vegetable spray and bring up to medium-high heat. Toss in the cabbage, snow peas, sprouts, water chestnuts, soy sauce, garlic, and scallions and sauté until the vegetables are soft and tender, about 8 to 10 minutes.

If there's a lot of liquid in the pan, drain the vegetables in a colander. Then scoop them into a large bowl and stir in the peanut butter. Let cool.

When you're ready, preheat the oven to 500°F. Lay out the egg roll skins and divide the filling among them, shaping little logs of it at one end of each skin. Roll each up firmly, surrounding the filling and tucking in the corners as you go. Brush the edges of the skins with the egg white to seal. Then set each egg roll on a cookie sheet that's been sprayed with nonstick vegetable spray. Paint each egg roll with peanut oil to coat. Then bake until burnished, about 12 minutes, flipping the egg rolls after 6 or 7 minutes. Serve warm.

On the Side

Side dishes can make or break the healthfulness of a meal: It doesn't take a nutritional genius to figure out that steamed broccoli is a smarter accompaniment to grilled salmon than French fries. So the focus of this chapter is on paying as much attention to what you serve with the entrée as you do to the main dish itself.

Our first recommendation is "think seasonal." In spring, for instance, asparagus is at its finest — and what could make a more perfect light accompaniment to poached fish? Similarly, if you're cooking up a spicy autumn chili, think of a robust in-season accompaniment, like baked winter squash.

Along with seasonality, be aware of taste and aroma. Strive for a full range of flavors and you'll be less tempted to reach for fatty toppings like sour cream. Garlic-scented sautéed greens, for instance, can liven up roast chicken in ways that a simple baked potato cannot.

Color figures in, too. You want side dishes that add visual interest. When you add a bundle of steamed julienned carrots to the chicken and sautéed greens, your eyes will feel as tantalized as your palate.

We've used these basic principles, along with others you'll find in this chapter, to create an array of side dishes: Lowfat savory grain dishes; crisp potatoes and other vegetables sautéed sans fat; slim potato salads; and high-flavor, low-calorie vegetable accompaniments such as unsalted cucumber pickles. You'll even discover how to vary your diet healthfully with those unusual vegetables that have been cropping up in your local produce section.

All Steamed Up

To cut fat and calories, steam chopped onion instead of sautéing in oil or butter. The result is onions that are sweet and aromatic.

BARLEY PILAF

4 SERVINGS

A wonderful accompaniment to roasted capon or turkey, or stuff into cored, steamed sweet peppers.

> *1 medium onion, chopped*
> *1 shallot, peeled and thinly sliced*
> *2 cloves garlic, peeled and thinly sliced*
> *boiling water for steaming*
> *²/₃ cup of pearled barley, uncooked*
> *1¼ cup chicken stock*
> *2 tablespoons freshly squeezed lemon juice*
> *1 bay leaf*

Steam the onion, shallot, and garlic over boiling water until just tender, about 4 to 5 minutes. (If your steamer has large holes, use a fine mesh strainer instead.)

Meanwhile, preheat a medium cast-iron or other heavy-bottomed saucepan over medium-high heat. When the pan is hot, pour in the barley and stir constantly, until golden brown. Then add the steamed onion, shallot, and garlic, the stock, lemon juice, and bay leaf. Bring to a boil, then reduce the heat, cover and simmer until all the liquid is absorbed, about 30 minutes.

Variations: Substitute other grains for the barley. Millet or quinoa, for instance, are nice in warm weather, and buckwheat or wheat berries are warming in winter. Rice pilaf, of course, is great any time. Adjust the amount of water and the cooking time according to package directions.

Bursting with Flavor

Sun-dried tomatoes are to tomatoes what raisins are to grapes. Those packed without salt, plain or jarred in olive oil, are best. To use, simmer in a bit of stock or dry white wine until soft, then chop and add to salads, omelettes, pasta, or sautés. Their flavor is so sparkling that no salt is needed.

COUSCOUS WITH TOMATOES AND MUSHROOMS

4 SERVINGS

Delicious with grilled salmon or tuna.

1½ cups chicken stock
1 cup couscous
splash olive oil
5 sun-dried tomatoes (packed without salt), finely chopped
3 dried porcini or other flavorful mushrooms, chopped
juice and pulp of 1 lemon
1 tablespoon sherry vinegar or other robust vinegar
1 tablespoon olive oil
3 scallions, minced

Bring the stock to a boil over medium heat in a medium saucepan; add the couscous, splash of olive oil, tomatoes, and mushrooms. Stir once, cover, remove from heat and let sit for about 5 minutes, or until all the water is absorbed.

Meanwhile, in a small bowl combine the lemon juice and pulp, vinegar, and the tablespoon of olive oil; whisk well.

When the couscous is ready, pour on the lemon mixture and toss well to combine. The best way to do this, so the couscous doesn't get smashed, is to use flat paddles. Serve warm or at room temperature.

Currying Flavor

The Indian curry powders you buy at the supermarket are blends of as many as 20 different spices, but many contain salt or stay on the shelf so long that their flavors are bland. Instead of spicing them up with salt or fatty ingredients, make your own curry powder.

CURRY POWDER

Into a mortar or electric spice grinder, add

- 1 teaspoon cumin
- 1 teaspoon corriander seed
- ½ teaspoon fenugreek seed
- pinch each of cardamon, cinnamon, celery seed, tumeric and black or red pepper

Grind until you have a smooth powder. Use in marinades, vegetable sautés, or potato salads.

Note: To release flavors, curry powder should be heated before eating.

CURRIED BROWN RICE DRESSING

4 SERVINGS
OR ENOUGH TO STUFF AN 8-POUND BIRD

2 cups cooked brown rice
1 tablespoon peanut oil or margarine
1 tablespoon apple juice concentrate
½ to 1 teaspoon curry powder, or to taste
1 small onion, chopped
1 tart apple, cored and finely chopped
1 egg white, beaten for about 20 seconds

Preheat the oven to 350°F.

Spread the rice in a 1½-quart casserole dish that's been sprayed with nonstick vegetable spray. Set aside.

Heat a large nonstick sauté pan over medium heat and add the peanut oil or margarine. When the oil is warm and fragrant (or the margarine has melted) add the apple juice concentrate and curry powder; stir to combine.

Toss in the onion and apple and sauté until tender, about 5 minutes. Pour over the rice and stir well, adding in the egg white as you go. Cover and bake until cooked through, about 25 to 30 minutes. Serve warm.

Rating the Rices

Whoever said it first was right! Rice is nice. We've long known that it's fun to eat, and it's now in the spotlight because its healthfulness has become so clear. Depending on the variety, a half-cup of cooked rice has a mere 82 to 89 calories and is virtually free of the notorious trio that is the bane of so many Western dishes — cholesterol, sodium, and fat.

There are about 7,000 known strains of rice, and it's a dietary staple for over half the people in the world. To narrow your choices to manageable proportions, we'll name just six that we suggest you explore:

- *Short-grain rice:* Used in making sushi, this rice is also popular for breakfast in many Chinese cuisines and is used to make noodles and dumpling doughs in Southeast Asian cooking. The grains are fat and round when cooked, and the rice is sticky and a bit heavy. Try it in a savory rice custard, but note that it's too sticky to mold.
- *Long-grain rice:* The world's favorite! It's famous in the cuisines of Greece, Spain, Italy, the Middle East, the Caribbean, Central and South America, North Africa, and the United States. Long-grain rice is about five times as long as it is wide and when cooked becomes light and separate, not sticky. Use it in pilafs, dressings, salads, casseroles, and paellas.
- *Medium-grain rice:* A good all-purpose rice, medium-grain can be used in most recipes. In fact, it can be used in place of long-grain rice by cutting back slightly on the amount of cooking water. Note that while it's less expensive than long-grain, it's also plumper and stickier.
- *Aromatic rice:* Most of these varieties have thin grains and fabulous aromas. Some smell like roasting nuts, others like popped corn, and a couple of varieties, which are popular in Southeast Asian cuisines, smell like lilacs or jasmine. These luscious aromas make for flavor without needing a grain of salt. Of the various types of aromatic rices, the most common include texmati, pecan, dainty, and wehani (a brown aromatic rice with huge reddish grains). Except for wehani, aromatic rices are delicate and cook in a short time. Flavor them with chilies or curries, but avoid using in dressings and casseroles because the grains are too fragile.
- *Arborio rice:* Here's the rice that put Italian risotto on the map. The grains are short and plump and take at least three times as much cooking liquid as grain. The result, however, is creaminess without cream.
- *Brown rice:* Health-wise, brown rice is king. It's similar to white rice, but unlike the latter it still has all seven of its bran layers intact. As a result, it has more fiber. We prefer the medium- or long-grain types of brown rice; short grain is a bit gluey. The grains in brown rice pop open during cooking, making it pleasantly nutty and chewy. Note that brown rice has a shelf life of only six months because of the extra bran layers. Smell before you buy to check for freshness.

BEANS AND RICE
WITH TOASTED PINE NUTS

4 SERVINGS

This dish is especially nice to serve with grilled vegetables, such as eggplant, or with poached chicken.

1½ cups water
¾ cups long- or medium-grain rice
1 cup cooked white or red beans
2 teaspoons olive oil
1 teaspoon basil
2 tablespoons pine nuts
2 scallions, minced

Bring the water to a boil in a medium saucepan and pour in the rice. Stir once and continue to boil, uncovered, for 5 minutes. Then reduce the heat to low, cover, and let simmer until cooked through, about 17 minutes (27 minutes for brown rice).

When the rice is cooked, stir in the beans, olive oil, and basil.

Toast the pine nuts by heating a dry nonstick sauté pan over medium heat. Toss in the pine nuts and stir constantly until lightly browned, about 2 minutes. This will give them a rich taste without your having to add butter.

Sprinkle the toasted nuts and the scallions over the rice and serve warm.

For flavor and fiber, leave the skins on spuds. Be sure to scrub them well and cut away any eyes or green patches before cooking.

ROASTED POTATOES WITH THYME

4 SERVINGS

A delicious accompaniment to barbecued foods or as a substitute for French fries.

> *1 pound new or other waxy-type potatoes*
> *2 teaspoons olive oil*
> *handful of fresh thyme sprigs, or 1½ teaspoons dried thyme*

Preheat the oven to 425°F.

Cut the potatoes into 2-inch pieces. If the potatoes are tiny, this may just mean halving them. Regardless, be sure some of the flesh is exposed.

Put the potatoes in a large baking pan and toss well with the olive oil, making sure all the potatoes are well coated and not overlapping. Then sprinkle on the thyme.

Roast in the center of the oven, uncovered, until the potatoes are soft inside and burnished, about 30 minutes. Serve warm.

Variation: Add a clove of peeled and thinly sliced garlic, along with the thyme.

Crispiny Foods without Deep Frying

The first secret of making crispy foods without lots of fat is to choose an oil that has a high smoking point. Canola and avocado oil are good on this count. The result is that fried foods will have the cooking time and temperature needed to become crisp on the outside yet meltingly soft on the inside. The second secret is to use a well-seasoned cast-iron pan; it has a heavy bottom that distributes heat evenly so foods can crisp without burning.

CRISP POTATOES WITH ROSEMARY

4 SERVINGS

1 pound new or other waxy-type potatoes
boiling water
1 tablespoon canola or avocado oil
2 sprigs fresh rosemary, or 1 teaspoon dried

Cut the potatoes into thin slices, then steam over boiling water until barely tender, about 5 minutes.

Meanwhile, preheat a well-seasoned cast-iron skillet over medium-high heat. When it's warm, add the oil and heat until warm, too.

When the potatoes are ready, pat them dry and arrange them in the skillet. Reduce the heat to medium, sprinkle on the rosemary, and let the potatoes cook, unstirred, until browned, about 4 minutes. Use a spatula to flip the potatoes and continue to cook until the second side has browned. Serve warm.

Sour Substitute

Combinations of lowfat dairy products can be healthy and delicious stand-ins for sour cream. Lowfat cottage cheese pureed with plain lowfat yogurt is a good place to start. Use your imagination to discover combinations of your own.

FLUFFY STUFFED POTATOES

4 SERVINGS

2 medium potatoes, baked
¼ cup lowfat cottage cheese
2 tablespoons part-skim ricotta cheese
3 tablespoons skim milk
1 tablespoon freshly grated parmesan or sapsago cheese
1 tablespoon minced fresh chives
paprika for sprinkling

Preheat the broiler.

Slice the potatoes in half lengthwise. Then scoop out the pulp of each half, leaving enough pulp so that a shell remains to hold the filling.

Beat the cottage and ricotta cheese together with a hand mixer. Add the potato pulp and skim milk, continuing to beat until the filling is fluffy.

Spoon the filling into the potato shells and top with the parmesan, chives, and paprika.

Broil until heated through and golden on top, about 2 to 3 minutes.

Hold the Mayo

To make a potato salad for four, you'd probably use 3 tablespoons of mayonnaise, adding 75 calories to each serving in the process. Instead, to cut calories and fat, use only 1 tablespoon of mayo combined with 1 stiffly beaten egg white.

Potassium and Potatoes

Surveys link high potassium intake to better resistance to strokes. Potatoes are high in potassium, but this mineral can be lost during processing and cooking. To preserve potassium, try microwaving fresh potatoes. The shortened cooking time will help retain the nutrients that nature put in.

Better without the Butter

Certain new varieties of potatoes look and taste buttery without any butter at all. Try Yellow Finnish, Yellow Rose, or Yukon Gold.

SLIM POTATO SALAD

4 SERVINGS

1 pound new or other waxy-type potatoes
2 tablespoons water or chicken stock
1 apple, cored and minced
1 small purple onion, minced
1 tablespoon reduced-calorie mayonnaise
2 tablespoons plain lowfat yogurt
½ teaspoon dried dill weed

Dice the potatoes. To microwave, arrange them in a micro-wave ring pan and sprinkle on 2 tablespoons of water or stock. Cover with vented plastic wrap and microwave on full power until tender, about 4½ minutes. Let stand for 4 minutes. If you don't have a microwave, steam the potatoes over boiling water until tender, about 12 to 15 minutes.

Pat the potatoes dry, but don't let them cool completely. Put them in a large bowl and toss in the apple and onion.

In a small bowl fold together the mayonnaise, yogurt, and dill weed. Scoop over the potatoes and toss to combine. Serve warm or at room temperature.

Variations

• Substitute cooked diced carrot for part of the potatoes
• Use 1 tablespoon minced fresh mint instead of the dill weed
• Instead of the purple onion, use minced fresh chives

Cancer-Fighting Vegetables

Vegetables high in vitamin A may help protect you from certain types of cancer; to date, more than a dozen studies support the link. Dark greens are among the best sources of vitamin A. Among your many choices are kale, spinach, chard, broccoli rabe (rapini), and bok choy leaves.

GREENS WITH GARLIC

4 SERVINGS

Serve with grilled chicken or toss with just-cooked pasta.

1 pound kale or other dark greens
2 teaspoons olive oil
2 cloves garlic, very finely minced
1 tablespoon freshly grated sapsago or parmesan

Trim tough stems from the greens, then shred the leaves into ribbons. The easiest way to do this is to stack up a bunch of leaves, roll them into a cigar shape, and start slicing at the end of the roll.

Meanwhile, warm the olive oil over medium-high heat in a well-seasoned cast-iron skillet or a nonstick sauté pan. Toss in the greens and garlic and sauté until just wilted and the color has brightened, about 2 to 3 minutes.

Sprinkle on the cheese and toss lightly. Serve warm.

Indispensable Ingredient

┃┃┃ No healthy gourmet should be without roasted sweet peppers. Their flavor is rich and robust without a trace of added fat, calories, or salt. To roast peppers, halve, core, and seed them. Then set under a broiler and char them on all sides. Next, set them in a paper bag, which will help steam the skins off. When cool, use your fingers and a paring knife to remove the skins. To use, slice and add to sautés, marinated vegetable salads, or pilafs.

BRAISED LEEKS WITH ROASTED RED PEPPERS

4 SERVINGS

Wonderful as an accompaniment to pasta, omelettes, or a frittata. Also great with poached fish or as an appetizer.

> *6 large leeks or 8 medium-small ones*
> *1 cup chicken stock*
> *¼ cup dry white wine*
> *3 bay leaves*
> *1 teaspoon marjoram*
> *1 teaspoon prepared dijon-style mustard*
> *2 roasted sweet red peppers, julienned*

Trim the leeks of their tough green parts and remove the roots. Then slice lengthwise into quarters. Rinse carefully to remove all sand, but don't let the petals separate.

Meanwhile, in a large sauté pan, bring the stock, wine, bay leaves, and marjoram to a boil. Set the leeks in carefully, cover, and reduce to a gentler simmer. Let the leeks braise until tender, about 5 minutes.

Use a slotted spoon to remove the leeks from the braising liquid, and set them on a large serving platter or individual plates. Bring the braising liquid back to a boil, whisking in the mustard as you go. Let the liquid reduce by about half, which will take about 3 minutes. Then pour it over the leeks. Sprinkle on the peppers and serve warm or at room temperature.

In a Pickle?

While your favorite pickle may appear innocent, it's probably loaded with salt. Why not make your own salt-free version with our easy marinade?

CRISP CUCUMBER PICKLES

MAKES ABOUT 2 CUPS

2 large cucumbers
⅓ cup rice vinegar or other mild white vinegar
1 tablespoon freshly squeezed lemon juice and pulp
2 teaspoons canola oil or mild olive oil
1 teaspoon prepared dijon-style mustard
1 clove garlic, peeled and very finely minced
3 tablespoons very finely minced fresh dill or
    1 teaspoon dried dill
freshly ground black pepper

Peel the cucumbers and halve vertically. Use a teaspoon to scoop out the seeds, then slice thinly.

In a large nonreactive bowl whisk together the vinegar, lemon juice and pulp, oil, and mustard. Stir in the garlic, dill, and pepper and mix well; add the cucumber slices.

Let marinate, refrigerated, overnight. The pickles will keep, covered and refrigerated, for about 10 days.

Microwaving Preserves Nutrients

Because less liquid is used and cooking time is shorter, microwaving vegetables helps minimize vitamin and mineral losses that occur during cooking. What's more, color and flavor are also retained, which means you don't need fatty sauces to make your vegetables appealing.

Ancient Chinese Secret

To maximize natural flavor, the Chinese cut their vegetables on a severe diagonal before cooking. Exposing more surface reveals more flavor. Take advantage of Chinese wisdom with carrots, parsnips, celery, asparagus, and broccoli stems.

BROCCOLI WITH SHALLOTS

4 SERVINGS

¾ pound broccoli
1 medium shallot, peeled and very finely minced
2 tablespoons stock or dry white wine
endive petals or curly red lettuce for serving

Trim the tough ends off of the broccoli and discard. Cut off the florets and set aside. If the stems are unusually tough, peel them; then slice the stems into thin diagonals and toss them into a ring pan, and add the shallot and stock. Cover with vented plastic wrap and microwave on full power for about 1 minute. Meanwhile, trim the florets into even sizes.

Add the broccoli florets to the cooked stems, shallots, and stock, re-cover and continue to microwave until tender, about 2 minutes. Let stand for 3 minutes. Then drain and serve warm or at room temperature on endive petals.

Variation: Toss drained warm broccoli with a low-oil vinaigrette and let marinate for at least an hour. Serve at room temperature.

Great Grilling

When it comes to grilling, many people think only of meats. But vegetables are delicious when grilled, and the burnished taste and texture allow for lively flavor without adding rich sauces. Summer squash, eggplant, corn on the cob, peppers, and tomatoes are among the best grillers. Except for the tomatoes, all should be blanched first. If you can't grill, try broiling.

GRILLED SQUASH

4 SERVINGS

1¼ pound summer squash or zucchini, about 7 inches long
boiling water for blanching
1 tablespoon very finely minced fresh basil
   or ½ teaspoon dried
2 teaspoons freshly grated sapsago or parmesan cheese

Prepare the grill.

Trim the squash and slice lengthwise into ½-inch slices. Set the slices in a large strainer. Blanch by pouring boiling water over the slices for about 7 seconds. Pat the slices dry, then arrange them on the grill with the rack about 4 inches from the heat.

Let the slices grill until spotted with brown, about 3 minutes. Then flip and let the second side brown. Remove the slices from the grill and immediately sprinkle with the basil and cheese. Serve warm with poached fish, or grilled beef or lamb.

Variations:
- If grilling is inconvenient, set the vegetables on a cake-cooking rack, place the rack on a cookie sheet, and broil.
- Instead of basil and cheese, garnish the slices with fresh tomato sauce.

Magic Mustard

Use prepared mustard, teaspoon for teaspoon, to replace the salt in sauces. Lighter mustards, such as dijon-style, are nice with sauces for vegetables and fish; coarse, country-style mustards are good with more robust sauces.

ASPARAGUS WITH MUSTARD SAUCE

4 SERVINGS

1 cup chicken stock
1 tablespoon white wine vinegar
1 pound fresh asparagus
1 tablespoon margarine or sweet butter
1 tablespoon instant flour
1 teaspoon prepared dijon-style mustard
freshly ground black pepper

Snap off—never cut—the tough ends of each asparagus spear and discard.

In a large nonreactive sauté pan over medium heat whisk together the stock and vinegar. Drop in the asparagus, using a chopstick or a roll of foil to prop up the tender tips. Cover loosely and poach until tender, about 4 to 5 minutes, depending on the thickness of the spears.

Using a slotted spoon or tongs, remove the spears from the liquid and place in a serving dish; cover with paper towels, foil, or a clean dish towel to keep warm.

Add the margarine or butter, flour, mustard, and pepper to the liquid, whisking constantly over medium heat. (By using the cooking liquid to make the sauce, you've captured all the B and C vitamins that have been cooked out of the vegetables.) Continue to whisk until the sauce has thickened, about 3½ minutes.

Serve the sauce warm, spooned over the asparagus.

Healthy Sauces and Tosses

Start with the freshest vegetables possible, then steam, blanch, or microwave until tender. But don't reach for the butter or sour cream. Instead, try one of these delicious and lean ideas:

Carrots: Pat still-warm carrots dry, then toss with a mixture of plain lowfat yogurt, dill, and freshly grated lemon zest.

Acorn squash: Drizzle still-warm chunks with a splash of dry sherry, freshly grated ginger, and minced fresh chives.

Green beans: Toss with an herbed vinegar, such as tarragon, and a splash of olive oil.

Brussels sprouts: Finely chop a rich, ripe tomato, then mix in a minced scallion. Toss with sliced still-warm sprouts.

Garden peas: Sauté sliced mushrooms and minced shallot in a bit of olive oil in a nonstick pan. Then toss with just-cooked peas.

Beets: Sprinkle still-warm chunks or slices with freshly squeezed lemon juice and pulp and a pinch of freshly grated nutmeg.

Corn: Combine just-cooked kernels with minced sweet red pepper, mild green chilies, and minced purple onion.

Cauliflower: Toss still-warm florets with the juice and pulp of a freshly squeezed lime, minced fresh dill, and a splash of peanut oil.

Cabbage: Toast caraway seeds in a nonstick pan, then add to a bit of plain lowfat yogurt. Toss with still-warm florets.

Four Ways to Sauté Sans Fat

- Add fresh lemon slices to a hot nonstick pan. Then toss in vegetables and sauté. Use 3 to 4 lemon slices for each ¾ pound of sliced or chunked vegetables.
- Heat a small amount of hot stock or dry white wine in a nonstick pan. Then add the vegetables and sauté over medium-high heat until tender. You'll need about 3 tablespoons of stock or wine for each ¾ pound of sliced or chunked vegetables.
- Sauté vegetables with sliced or minced fresh mushrooms. The liquid the mushrooms give off will create a steaming effect on the other veggies.
- Summer vegetables such as zucchini are delicious when sautéed in a bit of tomato juice. You'll need about 3 tablespoons of juice for ¾ pound of sliced zucchini. Sprinkle with minced fresh chives before serving.

Relishes to Relish

- Combine steamed minced sweet potatoes with minced sweet red pepper and just a few very finely minced pecans. Toss with a bit of cider vinegar and a splash of peanut oil. Serve with roasted turkey or chicken.
- Combine chopped tart apple with minced onion and a bit of prepared horseradish. Stir in a small amount of plain lowfat yogurt or reduced-calorie mayonnaise. Serve with roasted lamb or steamed shrimp, lobster, or crab.

Vegetables Mom Never Knew

Weary of the same old spinach? Can't bear another carrot? Then look around your produce department and discover some new varieties of vegetables. There are lots of healthful alternatives that make vegetable eating more interesting and varied. Here are four that are available at most supermarkets.

Jicama (HEE-kah-mah): This tuber looks like a large, round potato but tastes like a crisp water chestnut. It's popular in Caribbean and Mexican cuisines, where it is peeled, chunked, and simmered in fish stews. Because it's so low in fat and calories, it makes a great replacement for fatty chips with dips. Simply peel and slice. ½ cup contains about 25 calories.

Chayote (kie-OH-tee): This pear-shaped, pale green squash is also called *mirliton* (Arcadian) and *shoo-shoo* (Brazilian). The taste is delicate and a bit zucchinilike; it's great halved, stuffed, and baked like acorn squash. Brazilians peel and chunk shoo-shoo, then sauté it with garlic and plump shrimp. The best news of all is that ½ cup of this sensational squash has a mere 20 calories.

Yard-long beans: Although really just 18 inches long, these beans from Asia are not short on taste. They can be cooked like regular green beans, and certain Chinese legends say that eating them while long, without cutting, will bring good luck and longevity. We can't guarantee that, of course, but we're sure you'll find yard-longs to be an interesting change of pace from the normal green bean routine. Steam them, then, if you're superstitious, tie a knot in the middle of each bean before serving; otherwise slice on a sharp diagonal to size before steaming.

Broccoli rabe: This dark, leafy green is also called *rapini* (Italian) and flowering broccoli (Chinese). The leaves, stems, and little flower buds are all eaten. To prepare, chop and sauté in a bit of olive oil, or add to stir-fries. Broccoli rabe can even stand in for spinach and chard and, like these deep green vegetables, offers plenty of carotene—the plant form of vitamin A.

Perfect Poultry

Diet-conscious cooks will welcome the variety, flavors, and textures that poultry offers. Many birds, especially chicken and turkey, are naturally low in fat and blossom with light cooking techniques and ingredients. For instance, Lemon-Ginger Chicken combines ribbons of plump chicken sizzled with a savory lemon and ginger sauce—and it's so delicious we've been known to forget that there's absolutely no fat added.

One secret behind Lemon-Ginger Chicken and other lean recipes is our use of chicken cutlets, which are boneless, skinless chicken breasts. We will tell you how to pick them at their best or how to make your own. Then, as we illustrate, you can braise, stir-fry, broil, poach, grill, sauté, roast, or stuff cutlets deliciously.

We'll also fill you in on the secrets of no-fat-added roasting for whole birds, defatting duck, and a bouquet of low-calorie sauces and marinades, plus ideas that keep poultry luscious yet lean.

Skin Deep

Most of the fat in poultry lurks in and just around the skin. By removing poultry skin, you remove fat, but the tender flesh is now vulnerable to overcooking. The solution is to cook with a moist method, like braising, which imparts flavor to chicken and leaves it juicy.

SPICED AND FRAGRANT CHICKEN

4 SERVINGS

3¼ cups tomato sauce
4 chicken legs, skin removed
½ cup chicken stock
2 teaspoons good-quality curry powder
⅛ teaspoon cayenne, or to taste
2 cloves garlic, minced
freshly ground black pepper to taste
1½ cups fresh green peas

Heat the tomato sauce in a large saucepan on low heat. Add the chicken, stock, curry powder, cayenne, garlic, and black pepper. Cover and continue to simmer on low until the chicken is tender, about 1½ hours.

Use tongs and a fork to gently remove meat from the chicken legs. Return the meat to the sauce, add the peas, and simmer until the peas are tender, about 12 minutes.

Serve warm over an aromatic rice or tiny pasta, like orzo.

Poultry Particulars

Look for poultry that has creamy-pink, moist flesh that's springy and smells clean. Store in closed plastic bags in the coldest part of the refrigerator for up to two days or in the freezer for up to four months. We prefer fresh to frozen poultry, because fresh has more flavor. Nonetheless, frozen poultry retains good texture and can be useful when convenience counts.

LEMON-GINGER CHICKEN

4 SERVINGS

juice and pulp of 1 lemon
¾ teaspoon ground ginger
¾ pound chicken cutlet, cut into thin ribbons
¼ cup stock
1 tablespoon brown sugar
1 teaspoon cornstarch
1 scallion, very finely minced, for garnish

In a medium bowl combine the lemon, ginger, and chicken. Marinate for about 30 minutes.

Heat a wok or large nonstick sauté pan on medium-high, then pour in the stock. Lift the chicken from its marinade and add the chicken to the pan. Stir-fry until the chicken is cooked through; about 2½ minutes. Meanwhile, whisk the sugar and cornstarch into the marinade.

Make a well in the center of the chicken and pour in the marinade. Let it bubble and thicken slightly, then toss with the chicken. Garnish with the scallion and serve warm over skinny Chinese noodles or an aromatic rice.

Magic Marinades

Marinades can impart flavor without fat or salt, plus protect tender poultry flesh from becoming tough. Try flavored vinegars, herb mixes, and stocks as tasty replacements for conventional fatty marinades.

AFRICAN CHILI CHICKEN (CHICKEN PIRI-PIRI)

4 SERVINGS

juice and pulp of 1 lime
3 cloves garlic, mashed through a press
½ teaspoon chili powder, or to taste
1 teaspoon hot pepper sauce, or to taste
¾ pound chicken cutlets, separated into 4 pieces
*   and pounded to ¼-inch thick*
1 teaspoon peanut oil

In a flat glass baking dish combine the lime, garlic, chili powder, and hot pepper sauce. Place cutlets in the dish and allow to marinate for about 30 minutes, flipping after 15 minutes.

Heat a nonstick sauté pan on medium-high, then pour in the oil. When it's warm, add the cutlets and sizzle until cooked through, about 2½ minutes on each side. Serve warm with corn on the cob or corn bread.

Farewell to Fat

Another great way to prepare juicy no-fat-added chicken cutlets is in the microwave. A pound of boneless chicken cutlet, divided into four pieces, will take about 5½ minutes on full power, plus 5 minutes of standing time. It's great to keep on hand for chicken salads, sandwiches, or lowfat snacks.

QUICK CHICKEN WITH MARJORAM AND THYME

4 SERVINGS

2 tablespoons dry white wine
½ teaspoon thyme
½ teaspoon marjoram
¾ pound chicken cutlets, separated into 4 pieces
*   and pounded lightly*

Combine the wine, thyme, and marjoram in a 9-inch glass pie dish. Add the chicken, dipping both sides in the wine mixture. Nudge the chicken to the sides of the dish. Then cover with vented plastic wrap and microwave on full power until cooked through, about 5 minutes. Rotate the dish midway. Non-microwavers can sauté in a nonstick pan until cooked through, roughly 4 minutes per side.

Let stand for 5 minutes, then serve warm or very slightly chilled with a salad of interesting greens.

Homemade Cutlets

By skinning and boning chicken breasts you can easily make your own chicken cutlets. For turkey cutlets, simply skin a turkey breast and slice.

CHICKEN RIBBONS WITH BLUE CHEESE AND SPAGHETTI

4 SERVINGS

2 teaspoons olive oil
2 medium onions, peeled, thinly sliced, and separated into rings
1 sweet red pepper, cored, seeded, and julienned
¾ pound chicken cutlet, sliced into ribbons
¼ cup minced Italian flat-leaf parsley
½ cup dry white wine or chicken stock
¼ cup crumbled blue cheese
1½ cups cooked spaghetti

Heat a large nonstick sauté pan on medium-high, then pour in the oil. When it's warm add the onions, peppers, and chicken; cover loosely with a lid or crumpled foil and let simmer until the onion is tender and fragrant, about 10 minutes.

Add the parsley and wine and bring to a boil. Continue to boil for several minutes until the sauce has thickened slightly and the chicken is cooked through. The parsley will wilt slightly but should still be bright in color.

Toss with the cheese and spaghetti and serve warm.

The Skin Story

Despite all you've heard about fat in chicken skin, you can leave it on when grilling. The skin will protect the flesh from drying out and toughening from the intense heat. Just be sure to remove the skin before eating.

GARLIC-GRILLED CHICKEN

4 SERVINGS

The chicken (and garlic) are great served warm with crusty bread.

2 large chicken breasts, split
4 cloves garlic, peeled and thinly sliced
4 teaspoons coarse, country-type prepared mustard

Prepare the grill.

Gently loosen the skin from the chicken and divide the garlic slices among the pieces by tucking under the loosened skins. Rub each chicken piece with mustard.

Grill about 5½ inches from the heat until cooked through, about 9 minutes on each side. Be sure to remove the skin before eating.

Many traditional culinary techniques can be made more healthful with just a few modifications. Duxelles — finely chopped mushrooms that are normally sautéed in butter, often with a bit of shallot and tarragon, and used as a flavor enhancer for poultry and other foods — are a good example. Duxelles can become fat-free by sautéing them in a nonstick pan in their own juices. Use to enliven sauces or to garnish poached or grilled chicken.

MUSHROOM-STUFFED STEAMED CHICKEN

4 SERVINGS

¾ pound mushrooms, minced
1 shallot, minced
2 cloves garlic, peeled and minced
1 tablespoon dry sherry
1 teaspoon tarragon
1 egg white, beaten until just frothy
2 tablespoons freshly grated parmesan cheese
1 pound chicken cutlets, separated into 4 pieces
    and pounded to ¼-inch thick
boiling water for steaming

Heat a large nonstick sauté pan on medium-high and toss in the mushrooms, shallot, garlic, sherry, and tarragon. Sauté until the mushrooms are dark and fragrant and all the liquid has been absorbed, about 8 minutes. Let them cool slightly, then fold in the egg white and cheese.

Lay 4 sheets of plastic wrap on the counter and spread out a piece of chicken on each. Divide the mushroom stuffing into quarters and set each quarter on a piece of chicken. Use the back of a spoon to spread the stuffing out, then roll up each piece of chicken as you would a jelly roll; then roll the plastic wrap tightly around each roll, carefully folding in the corners of the plastic wrap. Set the rolls on a steamer over boiling water, cover, and steam until cooked through, about 15 minutes.

Unwrap, slice into disks, and serve warm or at room
temperature.

Nutritious Nuggets

Forgo those little chicken morsels you find at fast food
restaurants! By the time they come out of the fryer,
they're loaded with fat and high in sodium. Whip up our
healthy version instead—or try poached chicken cut into
chunks and dipped in a dilled yogurt sauce.

SAVORY CHICKEN BITES

4 SERVINGS

These little chicken bites travel well and make good snack and
picnic food.

1 pound chicken cutlets
2 cloves garlic, minced
1 teaspoon thyme
1 shallot, minced
2 teaspoon dijon-style prepared mustard
1 teaspoon olive oil
½ cup chicken stock
1 bay leaf

Cut the chicken into manageable pieces and toss them into a
food processor along with the garlic, thyme, shallot, and mustard. Process until the chicken is the texture of ground beef. (Or
combine in 2 batches in a blender.)

Wet your hands and shape the ground chicken into 1-inch
balls; set aside.

Heat a large nonstick sauté pan on medium and pour in the

oll. Add the balls and sauté until you can smell the thyme and garlic, about 2 minutes. Add the stock and bay leaf, bring to a boil, and simmer until cooked through, about 5 minutes, stirring often. Serve warm, at room temperature, or very slightly chilled.

CHICKEN CUTLETS WITH SAFFRON AND GREEN OLIVES

4 SERVINGS

2 teaspoons olive oil
1 teaspoon sweet butter or margarine
¾ pound chicken cutlets, separated into 4 pieces and
   pounded to ¼-inch thick
1 medium sweet onion, peeled and chopped
1 sweet red pepper, cored, seeded, and chopped
1 bay leaf
½ teaspoon saffron threads, crushed between the fingers
2 large ripe tomatoes, chopped
3 tablespoons chopped green olives

Heat the oil and butter in a large nonstick sauté pan until the butter has melted. Arrange the cutlets in the pan and toss in the onion, pepper, bay leaf, and saffron. Sizzle on medium until the chicken has cooked through, about 3 minutes on each side.

Add the tomatoes and olives; increase the heat to high and bubble until the tomatoes have wilted, about 3 minutes. Serve warm.

The Ultimate Irony

A well-seasoned cast-iron pan will give many foods a crisp texture without deep frying. Take enchiladas, for example. Traditionally cooked in lard, they cook to perfection in cast-iron using only a splash of olive oil.

CHICKEN ENCHILADAS

4 SERVINGS

Serve these crisp enchiladas with salsa or avocado on the side.

1 ripe tomato, cored, seeded, and chopped
½ teaspoon hot pepper sauce, or to taste
1 teaspoon oregano
½ teaspoon freshly ground cumin
2 cloves garlic, peeled and very finely minced
1 pound chicken cutlets, medium chopped
4 soft flour tortillas
¼ cup reduced-calorie Jack-type cheese, coarsely grated
1 teaspoon olive oil

Combine the tomato, hot pepper sauce, oregano, cumin, garlic, and chicken in a medium bowl and marinate for about 30 minutes. Then pour into a large nonstick sauté pan and sizzle on medium until the chicken is just cooked through, about 10 minutes.

Arrange a log shape of chicken on each tortilla. Sprinkle on the cheese and roll up. Preheat a well-seasoned cast-iron skillet and warm the oil in it. Set each enchilada seam side down in the skillet and cook on medium until the tortillas have begun to brown, about 2 to 3 minutes on each side. While the enchiladas are cooking, press down with a spatula from time to time.

There's more than one way to defat a duck. Here are three lean ideas:

- Start with a naturally lean variety of duck, such as Muscovy. Your poultry purveyor can order one for you.
- When roasting, use a raised roasting rack so the duck won't be sitting in a pan of fat as it cooks. Or try a vertical roaster, where the cavity of the bird fits over a standing wire rack and the fat drips out.
- Render fat out of a quartered duck before roasting by first microwaving for about 8 minutes. Then roast as usual, but cut the original cooking time in half.

ROAST DUCK WITH VERMOUTH AND ROSEMARY

4 SERVINGS

1 duck, about 5 pounds
1/3 cup dry white vermouth
1 tablespoon rosemary, minced

Use poultry shears to cut the duck into quarters, discarding the back and wings. Also cut out all the visible fat (you'll find a lot around the neck). Arrange the quarters in a microwave drainer with a drip dish to catch the fat. Cover and microwave on full power for about 8 minutes. Let stand for 5 minutes more.

Next, set the quarters in a flat, nonreactive dish and sprinkle on the vermouth and rosemary. Cover and let marinate for several hours. (Overnight is even better.)

Preheat the oven to 400°F. Arrange the quarters on a raised roasting rack with a drip pan underneath. Roast the duck until burnished and cooked through, about 35 minutes. Serve warm, and remove the skin before eating.

Lean Roasting for Whole Birds

To keep birds lean without adding fat, start them roasting at a high temperature — 450°F — to help lock the juices in. Roast at this temperature for about 10 to 15 minutes, then lower the temperature to 350°F. for the remainder of the cooking time. Check the internal temperature with a meat thermometer; when it reaches 170°F., the bird is ready. Since free-range poultry is leaner, it will take a bit less time than supermarket-bought birds.

CHILI-ROASTED CORNISH HENS

4 SERVINGS

½ cup plain nonfat yogurt
2 teaspoons chili powder
2 cloves garlic, mashed through a press
2 Cornish hens, split down the back to make 4 pieces

Preheat the oven to 450°F.

In a small bowl combine the yogurt, chili powder, and garlic. Rub it into the hens; then arrange hens on a raised roasting rack over a drip pan. Roast for about 10 minutes, then lower the temperature to 350°F. Continue to roast until cooked through, about 10 minutes more. Serve warm, at room temperature, or very slightly chilled.

- Always use a raised roasting rack to allow fat to drip away; An inch of water in the bottom of the catch pan will keep dripping fat from smoking during the long cooking. (This is good practice for all kinds of whole poultry.)
- Keep white meat moist without added fat by roasting turkey breast-side down.
- Baste the turkey with lean liquids, like apple juice or chicken stock seasoned with thyme.
- Let the turkey "relax" for about 20 minutes before carving. This will help keep it moist and juicy.
- Cook stuffing separately to maximize leanness. When cooked inside the turkey, stuffing can absorb considerable amounts of fat.

JULIENNE OF TURKEY WITH CHINESE PEAS

4 SERVINGS

2 teaspoons peanut oil
2 cloves garlic, peeled and smashed
2 slices fresh ginger, peeled
¾ pound turkey cutlets, sliced thinly against the grain
2 cups Chinese peas, with pods
boiling water for blanching
⅓ cup chicken stock
1 teaspoon reduced-sodium soy sauce
1 tablespoon dry sherry

Heat the oil along with the garlic and ginger in a wok over medium high heat. Sizzle for about 45 seconds until fragrant, taking care the garlic doesn't burn. Discard the garlic and ginger.

Add the turkey and stir-fry until cooked through, about 3 minutes.

Meanwhile, set the peas in a strainer over the sink, blanch by pouring water over for about 5 seconds. Pat dry and add to the turkey; toss well and remove from the heat.

In a small saucepan combine the stock, soy sauce and sherry. Boil until reduced by half, about 3 to 4 minutes. Pour the sauce over the turkey and peas and toss well. Serve warm with an aromatic rice.

Alternative Turkey

If you've only tried the whole bird or familiar turkey parts, it's time to become acquainted with some other fine choices. They make tasty lean substitutes for traditional beef steaks and fillets.

* *Turkey tenderloin* is to turkey what filet is to beef. It comes from the breast portion in pieces (about five to the pound) and is low in fat, low in calories, and very tender. Try it sautéed in a bit of olive oil with basil and thyme.
* *Turkey cutlets* also hail from the breast portion and are, essentially, raw sliced turkey breast. Try them marinated and grilled, stir-fried, or as a substitute for veal.

GRILLED TURKEY STEAK

4 SERVINGS

Serve with roasted potatoes and mixed greens.

> 1 tablespoon prepared dijon-style mustard
> 1 tablespoon finely grated onion
> ¾ pound turkey steak, about ½-inch thick

Prepare the grill.

Combine the mustard and onion in a small bowl and rub it into the turkey steak. Let marinate for about 30 minutes, then grill until cooked through, about 5 minutes on each side.

TURKEY TENDERLOIN
WITH MUSHROOMS AND PORT

4 SERVINGS

¾ pound turkey tenderloin, pounded to ¼-inch thick
1 tablespoon flour
2 teaspoons olive oil
⅓ cup beef stock
2 tablespoons port wine
¼ cup minced mushrooms

Sprinkle the turkey with the flour. Meanwhile, heat the oil in a large nonstick sauté pan. Set in the turkey and sizzle on medium until cooked through, about 2½ minutes on each side. Remove the turkey from the pan and keep it warm.

Pour in the stock, port, and mushrooms; bring to a boil. Continue to boil until the mushrooms are soft and the liquid is reduced by half — about 3 to 4 minutes — stirring often. Pour the sauce over the turkey and serve warm.

Go Fish

No one's quite sure which came first—consumer demand for fresh, healthful fish or the unmistakable improvement in the quality and value of the fresh fish supply. But there can't be any doubt about the health benefits of fish.

You already know that most varieties are low in calories, low in fat, and offer valuable vitamins and minerals. What's more, fish contain special compounds called omega-3s, which have special heart-healthy properties and may even help combat psoriasis and rheumatoid arthritis. Most fish offer some omega-3s but cold-water fish, such as salmon and mackerel, tend to be the richest sources.

How sad that these health benefits are sometimes undermined by deep-frying fish or smothering it in fatty sauces. We find that really fresh fish is best prepared simply, so that delicate tastes and textures are enhanced rather than hidden.

Your senses are the key to choosing fresh fish. Start with your nose. Fresh fish smells clean and briny, not fishy. If you find yourself in a market that smells fishy, leave. Next, use your eyes. Filets and steaks should have clear color and look moist. Whole fish should have bright red or pink gills and clear, gently bulging eyes. Now touch. If possible, poke the fish with your finger. The flesh should be springy.

At home, wrap fresh fish in waxed paper so it can breathe and leave it in the coldest part of the refrigerator for up to two days. Shellfish such as mussels, clams, crabs, oysters, and lobster should be cooked as soon as possible.

Our recipe files contain an ocean of lowfat, low-calorie ideas on ways to prepare, sauce, and serve fish. Here we present those that make the most of its taste, texture, and healthfulness.

Keeping Lean Fish Lean

Complement fish with lowfat accompaniments like steamed or sizzled vegetables instead of fatty cream sauces. Steamed and julienned carrots and leeks are great tossed over flounder or scallops, for instance, and the fish itself is low in saturated fat.

PAN-GRILLED MARLIN WITH FRIZZLED ONIONS

4 SERVINGS

2 large sweet onions, peeled, sliced, and separated into rings
2 teaspoons Worcestershire sauce
2 teaspoons olive oil, divided
1 pound marlin steak, 1-inch thick
juice and pulp of ½ lime
pinch ground cumin seed

In a large bowl toss together the onions, Worcestershire, and 1 teaspoon of the olive oil.

Preheat a heavy-bottomed sauté pan on high, then tip in the onion mixture. Reduce the heat to medium and sauté until the onions are browned and frizzled, about 5 to 6 minutes. Remove from the pan and keep them warm and handy.

Adjust the heat to medium-high. Then rub the marlin with the lime, remaining teaspoon of olive oil, and cumin. Set the marlin in the pan and sear for 30 seconds. Then flip and let it cook for about 3 minutes, pressing occasionally with a spatula. Flip and continue to cook for about 3 minutes more. Marlin, which many people feel tastes like pork, will become fibrous if overcooked, so take care. Serve hot, topped with the onions.

Sensational substitutions: Halibut, salmon steak, swordfish, tuna steak, or shark.

Cast to Last

A well-seasoned cast-iron skillet is a great way in which to cook fish without adding extra fat or calories. The heavy bottom keeps the fish from burning while allowing it to sear on the outside. This leaves the fish moist and tender within.

GINGER-GLAZED FRESH TUNA

4 SERVINGS

Great with steamed green beans or Chinese peas.

2 teaspoons regular or reduced-sodium soy sauce
1 teaspoon grated fresh ginger
1 tablespoon dry sherry
1 teaspoon orange juice concentrate
1 pound tuna steak, sliced to ½-inch thick
2 teaspoon peanut oil
2 scallions, very finely minced

Preheat a well-seasoned cast-iron skillet on medium-high. This will take 4 to 5 minutes.

Meanwhile, in a small bowl, combine the soy sauce, ginger, sherry, and orange juice concentrate. Rub it into the tuna.

Pour the oil into the skillet and reduce the heat to medium. Use a slotted spoon to lift the tuna out of the marinade and set it in the skillet. Let it cook for about 1½ minutes. Flip, add the scallions and marinade, and continue to cook for about another 1½ minutes. To serve, arrange the tuna on a serving plate or individual plates. Then use a spatula to scrape up the marinade and scallions and sprinkle over the tuna.

Sensational substitutions: Instead of tuna try swordfish, marlin, shark, salmon steak, or halibut.

Better to Blanch

Because of the low fat content, many fish can be difficult to grill. Typically, these fish become tough on the outside before the inside is ever cooked. The high heat is the culprit, but you can solve the problem without smothering the once-lean fish in fat in order to protect it. Instead, blanch it briefly (as described in the recipes following) before grilling. This sets the protein without toughening the fish or adding a single calorie.

GRILLED MONKFISH

4 SERVINGS

Serve warm with a colorful vegetable like roasted sweet peppers, or chilled and thinly sliced with mixed greens.

> 1 pound monkfish
> (buy it butterflied, so it's no thicker than 1½ inches)
> 1 teaspoon prepared dijon-style mustard
> 1 tablespoon freshly squeezed lime juice
> ½ teaspoon dried dill weed

Prepare the grill.

Blanch the monkfish in bubbling water for about 2 minutes; or microwave, covered, on full power for about 1½ minutes.

Pat the fish dry, then rub the mustard, lime juice, and dill into it. Grill about 4 to 5 inches from the heat for about 5½ minutes on each side.

Sensational substitutions: Instead of monkfish, any steak-type fish will be great, especially tuna, cod steak, mahi mahi, swordfish, salmon steak or thick filet, halibut, and marlin. Delicate seafood, like sea scallops, can be blanched for about 30 seconds, secured in a grill basket, and grilled for about 1 minute on each side.

Smarter Sauces

In place of fatty sauces and marinades, use a low-oil vinaigrette. Choose one from our salad section, such as Orange-Cider Vinaigrette, or create your own.

MAHI MAHI BROCHETTES
WITH SESAME VINAIGRETTE

4 SERVINGS

Delicious with steamed broccoli and sautéed mushrooms.

> *1 pound mahi mahi, cut to 1-inch pieces*
> *juice and pulp of 1 lime*
> *1 tablespoon rice vinegar or other mild white vinegar*
> *1 teaspoon toasted sesame oil*
> *pinch dry mustard*

Scoop the mahi mahi pieces into a strainer and blanch in bubbling water for about 1 minute. You can also microwave them, covered, on full power for about 1 minute.

Meanwhile, in a medium bowl whisk together the lime juice, vinegar, oil, and mustard. When the fish is ready, pat it dry and toss with the marinade. Let marinate for about 1 hour.

Prepare the grill or broiler. Then thread the mahi mahi onto skewers. Grill or broil about 4 inches from the heat source until cooked through, about 3 minutes on each side, basting frequently with the marinade. Serve warm.

Sensational substitutions: Instead of mahi mahi, try any fish that won't fall apart when cut and skewered. Swordfish, salmon steak, monkfish, or shark will work well. Medium to large shrimp also work well, but cut the grilling time by about half.

Up-Scale Meat

Many cooks are discovering that their favorite steaks come from the fish market. Meaty fish, especially tuna, swordfish, and salmon steaks, have awakened many a beef lover to the delights of fish. Of course, the low saturated fat content of these fish is important, too!

Foiled Again

A great way to keep fish juicy and tender without adding fat is to bake it in a packet of foil or parchment paper. Add such aromatics as carrot, onion, and garlic (perfect with haddock), and you'll find you have no need for salt, either.

SALMON IN A PACKET

4 SERVINGS

1 pound salmon filet
2 stalks celery (leaves, too), chopped
2 cloves garlic, peeled and thinly sliced
1 shallot, peeled and thinly sliced
1 sweet red or yellow pepper, cored and julienned
4 sprigs fresh dill or 1 teaspoon dried dill weed

Preheat the oven to 400°F.

Set the salmon skin side down in the middle of a large sheet of heavy foil and sprinkle on the celery, garlic, shallot, pepper, and dill. Close the foil, folding over the edges so you have a tight package.

Set the package on a cookie sheet for easy handling and bake until cooked through, about 30 minutes. To serve, lift the salmon out of the foil and set on a serving plate, leaving behind the liquid at the bottom. Arrange the vegetables over the salmon and serve warm. The salmon is also good chilled with an accompaniment of coarse country-style mustard.

Sensational substitutions: Instead of salmon, try haddock, red snapper filet, flounder, Spanish mackerel, small bluefish filet, pompano, fluke, bass filet, trout filet, or catfish filet.

Fan Mail for Your Flounder

Microwaving is a perfect way to cook fish without fat. Since microwaves produce moist heat, fish can't dry out as it might in a thermal oven. Even delicate fish like flounder, sole, fluke, and plaice emerge succulent and delicious.

FLOUNDER WITH VERMOUTH AND HERBS

4 SERVINGS

1 pound flounder filet
1½ tablespoons dry white vermouth or fish stock
½ teaspoon thyme
½ teaspoon basil

Arrange the flounder in a single layer in a microwave ring pan. If you don't have one, arrange the flounder around the edge of a 9-inch glass pie dish. Sprinkle on the vermouth and herbs. Then cover with vented plastic wrap and microwave on full power until cooked through, about 4½ minutes, rotating the dish midway. Let stand for about 4 minutes before serving warm.

Sensational substitutions: Instead of flounder, try haddock or any mild-flavor fish filet.

Smoke Signals

Small amounts of smoked fish can add lowfat flavor to fish salads, marinated vegetables, omelettes, and even mixed greens. The key is to use fish that has been smoked without salt (it's washed away before smoking) or preservatives. There are many brands from which to choose, and your local fish purveyor should be able to steer you in the right direction.

FRESH AND SMOKED SALMON SALAD

4 SERVINGS

¾ pound salmon filet or steak
2 ounces smoked salmon
2 scallions, very finely minced
2 tablespoons fresh parsley, stemmed
1 teaspoon capers
1 shallot, minced
2 teaspoons olive oil
2 tablespoons freshly squeezed lemon juice
watercress for serving

Set the salmon filet in a pan of gently bubbling water and cover. Poach until cooked through, about 12 minutes. Then remove from the water, drain, and pat dry. (You can also microwave the salmon filet, sprinkled with 1 tablespoon of water, covered, on full power for about 3 minutes. Let stand for 3 minutes before proceeding.)

If there's skin on the salmon (and there probably is) remove it. Then use your fingers to gently separate the salmon into chunks. Set them in a shallow mixing bowl.

Mince the smoked salmon and add it to the fresh salmon, along with the scallions.

Combine the parsley, capers, shallot, oil, and lemon juice in a spice grinder or mortar. Then whiz or pound until very smooth. Pour over the salmon and toss gently but well. Serve on beds of watercress.

Sensational substitutions: Instead of salmon, try fresh and smoked bluefish. You can also substitute poached fish of your choice for the fresh salmon.

Braising Is a Breeze

Braising is like poaching, except that the cooking liquid is used to make a final sauce. This gives the food a more complete flavor, cancelling out the need for salt.

BRAISED MACKEREL, CHINESE STYLE

4 SERVINGS

1 pound mackerel filets
1½ cups chicken or fish stock
1 tablespoon rice vinegar or other mild white vinegar
3 slices fresh ginger, peeled
3 cloves garlic, peeled and halved
2 teaspoons regular or reduced-sodium soy sauce
coarsey chopped scallions for serving

Arrange the mackerel filets skin side down in a large flat fry pan and add the stock, vinegar, ginger, garlic, and soy sauce. Bring to a boil and immediately reduce the heat to a simmer. Cover and continue to simmer until the mackerel is cooked through, about 10 minutes.

Use a large spatula to remove the mackerel from the braising liquid and gently set it on a serving platter. Now you can easily zip off and discard the mackerel skin.

Remove and discard the ginger and garlic from the braising liquid, then heat liquid on high until boiling. Continue to boil until the liquid has reduced by half, about 5 minutes. Pour the sauce over the fish and garnish with scallions before serving warm.

Sensational substitutions: Instead of mackerel, try any robust-flavored filet, especially salmon and red snapper.

Make Mine Mustard

Teaspoon for teaspoon, prepared mustard can be used in place of oils and other fats as a lowfat, low-calorie way of protecting delicate fish flesh during dry cooking. Keep a couple of bottles of interesting mustards on hand, such as herbed or dijon-style, and use a pastry brush to paint one on the fish before grilling, broiling, or sautéing. Of course, prepared mustards generally have salt that oils don't — something that the very strict sodium watcher must consider.

SALMON STEAK AU PÓIVE

4 SERVINGS

A French classic when served with roast potatoes.

> 2 teaspoons dijon-style mustard
> 1 pound salmon steak
> ½ teaspoon black peppercorns, or to taste
> ½ teaspoon white peppercorns, or to taste
> ½ teaspoon coriander seed

Paint the mustard on both sides of the salmon.

In a spice grinder or mortar, crush the peppercorns and coriander until they're medium-fine. Sprinkle the mixture on both sides of the fish and press in lightly with your hand. Then tuck in the thin tails of the salmon, so you have a roundish steak.

Spray a nonstick pan with nonstick vegetable spray and heat on medium. Set in the steaks and sizzle until cooked through, about 5 minutes on each side, pressing them down with a spatula from time to time. Serve warm.

Sensational substitutions: Instead of salmon, try swordfish, shark, fresh tuna, or cod steak.

Preferred Pan

A good-quality nonstick pan can make low-calorie, low-fat fish cooking a breeze. Choose a pan with a smooth surface that won't chip easily and a heavy bottom for even heat distribution. Fish filets work best with this method, so try flounder, snapper, haddock, or catfish and use a very small splash of oil (or nonstick vegetable spray), so the fish can slide in the pan.

RED SNAPPER
WITH MEXICAN VINAIGRETTE

4 SERVINGS

Nice with marinated zucchini and ripe tomato wedges.

> 1 pound snapper filet
> 2 tablespoons chicken or fish stock
> 2 tablespoons cider vinegar
> 1 tablespoon olive oil
> splash hot pepper sauce, or to taste
> ½ teaspoon chili powder, or to taste
> ½ teaspoon oregano
> pinch ground cumin
> pinch ground cloves

Spray a large nonstick sauté pan with nonstick vegetable spray and heat on medium. Set in the filets and when they just become fragrant (about 1 minute) pour in the stock. Sauté the filets until cooked through, about 3 to 4 minutes on each side.

Meanwhile, whisk together the vinegar, oil, hot pepper sauce, chili powder, oregano, cumin, and cloves. When the fish is finished, pour in the vinaigrette and let it sizzle for a second or two. Then remove the pan from the heat and serve fish warm.

Sensational substitutions: Instead of snapper, try haddock, flounder, grouper, catfish, trout filets, or bass filets.

Anchored in Tradition

Poaching has been around for so long that it's often over-
looked as an excellent no-fat-added cooking method. Fish
can be poached simply in a pan of bubbling water, but
adding aromatics will enable you to reduce salt as well as fat.
For instance, red snapper filets poached in tomato and lemon
juices will emerge delicious and full flavored.

COLD POACHED HADDOCK
WITH RED ONION AND DILL

4 SERVINGS

about 2 cups water
⅓ cup herbed vinegar
1 pound haddock
1 small red onion, peeled and finely chopped
¾ teaspoon dill weed
2 teaspoons olive oil
1 tablespoon freshly squeezed lemon juice

Pour the water and vinegar into a large, shallow nonreactive
fry pan and bring to a boil. Reduce the heat to a gentle simmer
and set in the haddock. Cover and poach until cooked through,
about 10 minutes. Use a large spatula to remove the haddock
from the poaching liquid to a flat, glass dish with sides. Discard
the poaching liquid.

In a small bowl combine the onion, dill weed, oil, and lemon
juice. Pour this over the haddock, cover, and refrigerate overnight. Serve very slightly chilled or at room temperature with
mixed greens.

Sensational substitutions: Instead of haddock, try flounder, sole,
bass filet, catfish, salmon filet, trout filet, red snapper filet, or
grouper.

Wholly Mackerel

Small- to medium-sized whole fish like mackerel, red snapper, trout, and bass can be steamed whole. The result is moist, tender fish without a trace of added fat; the fish skin acts as an automatic package that holds in natural juices.

WHOLE STEAMED TROUT

4 SERVINGS

Delicious with steamed asparagus. Or serve very slightly chilled with an assortment of interesting mustards and thinly sliced black bread.

2 whole trout, gutted, about ¾ pound each
4 scallions, coarsely chopped
1 lemon, thinly sliced

Prepare a steamer with about an inch of boiling water.

Use a sharp paring knife to make 3 slits in the fleshy part of each trout side. Do this on both sides.

Set the trout into the steamer and sprinkle on the scallions and lemon slices. Cover and steam until the trout is cooked through, about 10 to 12 minutes. Let the trout "relax" for about 5 minutes before fileting.

The Shell Game

Steamed clams, mussels, oysters, shrimp, lobster, crab, and scallops make great lowfat, low-calorie eating. Serve them for lunch, light dinner, and snacks with an assortment of raw or lightly steamed vegetables and a loaf of crusty bread. They can also be chopped and tossed with just-cooked pasta and a sprinkle of freshly grated parmesan cheese, or used as a garnish for tender mixed greens.

Clams and mussels can be microwaved easily. Simply arrange about a dozen around the edge of a large round dinner plate and sprinkle with a bit of lemon juice or dry white wine. Cover loosely with waxed paper and microwave on full power until open, about 2 minutes for the mussels and 3½ minutes for the clams. Serve as is or chop coarsely and add to soups.

The one thing you don't want to do with plump, delicious shellfish is to drown them in butter or other fatty sauces. From the culinary viewpoint, how anyone can take a rich, succulent chunk of lobster and dunk it in a bowl of fat is a mystery. And from the health side, who needs the fat?

In the event that your shellfish needs adornment, try nonfat flavorings such as squeezes of fresh lemon, lime, or orange. Here are some other ideas for bringing out the flavor, not the fat:

- Heat a bit of curry powder until fragrant in a dry, nonstick pan. Then fold into plain, lowfat yogurt. Great dotted on clams, oysters, and mussels or used as a dip for chunks of crab or lobster. You can also substitute chili powder for the curry powder — great served with shrimp.
- Mix a splash each of soy sauce, dry sherry, and cider vinegar into chicken or fish stock. Heat gently until just fragrant, then use as a dipping sauce for shrimp, crabmeat, scallops, or chunks of lobster.
- Dot oysters, clams, or mussels on the half-shell with a bit of low-oil pesto or salsa.
- Combine coarsely chopped fresh lemon (peel too), fresh parsley, and shallot in a processor or spice grinder and whiz until not quite smooth. This is called *gremolata*, and it's a wonderfully flavorful no-fat-added garnish to shellfish.

- Make a shellfish parfait by layering crabmeat, lobster or shrimp in parfait glasses with alternating layers of guacamole, herbed lowfat yogurt, marinated vegetables, or pasta salad.
- Combine equal parts chutney and lowfat yogurt or reduced-calorie mayonnaise. Use as a dipping sauce for scallops, shrimp, or crabmeat.

QUICK POACHED SHRIMP TO KEEP ON HAND

4 SERVINGS

These are a delicious addition to salads and make a great lowfat, low-calorie snack.

> *water for poaching*
> *2 tablespoons coriander seed or black peppercorns*
> *½ lemon, thinly sliced*
> *1 pound large shrimp, peeled and deveined*
> *splash toasted sesame oil*
> *2 teaspoons very finely minced fresh chives*

Bring the water to a gentle bubble in a large, flat fry pan. Add the coriander, lemon, and shrimp; cover and continue to bubble gently until the shrimp are pink and just beginning to curl, about 3 minutes.

Drain, pat dry, and toss with the sesame oil and chives. Enjoy warm or cover and keep refrigerated for up to 4 days.

Variation: Use olive oil instead of toasted sesame oil.

AROMATIC MUSSELS

4 SERVINGS

about 48 mussels, scrubbed and beards removed
2 cups fish or chicken stock
¼ cup dry white wine
juice and pulp of 1 lemon
1 tablespoon fennel seed
3 cloves garlic, peeled and thinly sliced

Arrange the mussels in a large, flat fry pan. Then pour on the stock and wine and sprinkle on the lemon, fennel, and garlic.

Cover and bring the mixture to a boil. Continue to boil until the mussels have opened, about 4 minutes. Discard any mussels that haven't opened after 5 minutes. To serve, arrange the mussels in shallow bowls and pour some aromatic liquid over each. Offer crusty bread for dunking.

Sensational substitution: Instead of mussels, try clams, but increase cooking time. Remember to discard any that haven't opened within a couple of minutes.

BAY SCALLOP SALAD
WITH SWEET PEPPERS AND SPINACH

4 SERVINGS

To maintain the silky texture (and natural lowfat properties) of these tender shellfish, steam them. Bay scallops can be done whole; larger sea scallops should be sliced into coins or quartered so they steam evenly throughout.

1 pound bay scallops
water for steaming
1 shallot, very finely minced
1 clove garlic, very finely minced
2 medium sweet peppers, cored and minced
  (you choose the colors)
½ pound spinach, washed well, stems removed,
  and leaves shredded
1 tablespoon cider vinegar
1 tablespoon olive oil
½ teaspoon coarse, country-style prepared mustard

Steam the scallops over the water until tender, about 2 minutes. Pat them dry and tip them into a large bowl. Add the shallot, garlic, peppers, and spinach; toss.

In a small bowl whisk together the vinegar, oil, and mustard. Pour over the scallop mixture and toss gently but well. Serve at room temperature. Nice with chilled orange wedges on the side.

Sensational substitutions: Instead of bay scallops, try quartered sea scallops, medium shrimp, or chunked salmon.

New Classics

With a little imagination, most classic recipes can be reduced in fat, calories, and salt. Quiche without the crust is a good example. So are fish soups and stews when freed of their fatty liquid and converted into light salads. To convert clam chowder and lobster stew into a delicious salad, for instance, use the usual seasonings, forget the heavy cream, and bind the salad with a combination of lowfat yogurt and reduced-calorie mayonnaise.

BOUILLABAISSE SALAD

4 SERVINGS

All you need in addition is a loaf of warm crusty bread.

2 teaspoons olive oil
1 small onion, peeled and chopped
1 small leek, cleaned, trimmed, and chopped
½ teaspoon each saffron, fennel seed, celery seed
¼ cup minced fresh parsley
pinch grated orange rind
¾ cup lobster meat, cooked
¾ cup shelled clams, cooked
¾ cup shelled mussels, cooked
¾ cup chunked haddock, cooked
1 tablespoon tomato sauce
2 tablespoons plain lowfat or reduced-calorie mayonnaise

Heat the olive oil in a large nonstick sauté pan. Then toss in the onion, leek, saffron, fennel, and celery seed. Sauté until the onion and leek are fragrant and barely wilted, about 4 minutes.

Scoop the onion mixture into a large bowl; add the parsley, orange rind, lobster, clams, mussels, and haddock.

In a separate small bowl combine the tomato sauce and yogurt. Then scoop into the salad and toss until all the fish is lightly coated. Serve at room temperature.

Variation: Any firm fish will work well, as long as you have 3 cups. Salmon, crab, and haddock are a good combination. You can even add a bit of smoked fish, if you wish.

Feel the Heat

A dash of hot pepper sauce or dried hot red pepper can lift flavors so much that you can cut down on fatty sauces. Hot pepper sauce is especially compatible with shrimp, catfish, red snapper, and crab.

SHRIMP WITH SPICY CURRY

4 SERVINGS

Serve with rice or pasta. Chilled apple wedges make a refreshing accompaniment.

> 1 tablespoon olive oil
> 2 cloves garlic
> 1 leek, cleaned, trimmed, and minced
> 1 small green pepper, cored and minced
> 2 tablespoons minced fresh parsley
> 1½ teaspoons curry powder, or to taste
> 1 pound medium shrimp, peeled and deveined
> 2 scallions, very finely minced

Heat the olive oil in a large sauté pan and add in the garlic, leek, green pepper, parsley, and curry powder. Sauté on medium until the vegetables are just tender and the curry is bold and fragrant, about 4 to 5 minutes. Immediately add the hot pepper sauce, shrimp, and scallions and sauté on high until the shrimp are cooked through, about 2 minutes.

Fish is famous in sauces for pasta and other foods, but so is the fat that goes with it. To reverse course and make these sauces lighter, concentrate on the fish and not the fat. For example, in lobster newburg, go heavy on the lobster and forget the cream, using milk instead. Pack more clams into clam sauce for linguini and sauté them in a nonstick pan with a bit of olive oil rather than the usual ½ cup of butter.

NEW ORLEANS SHRIMP
WITH CHILI SAUCE AND SPAGHETTI

4 SERVINGS

1 tablespoon olive oil
1 medium onion, chopped
½ cup dry white wine
1 cup chicken or fish stock
1 cup tomato sauce
1 teaspoon thyme
1 bay leaf
pinch cayenne pepper, or to taste
1 pound shrimp, peeled, deveined, and cooked
2 cups cooked spaghetti

Heat the olive oil in a large nonstick pan. Add the onion and sauté until fragrant and barely tender, about 3 minutes. Then add the wine, stock, tomato sauce, thyme, bay leaf, and cayenne; bring to a boil. Reduce the heat to a simmer and continue to cook until the sauce is fragrant and thick, about 10 minutes.

Add the shrimp and heat through. Toss with spaghetti and serve warm.

Note: If you like a more fiery flavor, add hot pepper sauce to taste.

Sensational substitutions: Instead of shrimp, try clams, mussels, or chunked haddock.

The Succulent Sauté

Delicate fish need to be protected during sautéing, or they will become tough and dry. Scallops and flounder filet are two fish that need special attention. Instead of using fat or oil to coat them, dust with flour, cornmeal, or oat bran and sauté in a nonstick pan over medium (no higher) heat.

SOFT SHELLED CRAB WITH FRESH THYME

4 SERVINGS

Great with corn on the cob.

2 teaspoons olive oil
½ cup cornmeal (you may not need it all)
8 small- to medium-sized soft shelled crabs
2 tablespoons minced fresh thyme or 1 teaspoon dried thyme
⅓ cup dry white wine or dry white vermouth
1 teaspoon dijon-style mustard

Heat the olive oil in a large nonstick sauté pan over medium heat.

Sprinkle the cornmeal over the crabs and pat down. The moisture on the crabs will hold the cornmeal. Add the crabs to the sauté pan and sauté until they've turned red and cooked through, about 2½ minutes on each side.

Arrange the crabs right side up on a serving platter and keep them warm. Then add the thyme, wine, and mustard to the sauté pan and bring to a boil, stirring constantly. Continue to boil until the sauce has thickened slightly and reduced by about a third. Pour the sauce over the crabs and serve warm.

Magnificent Meats

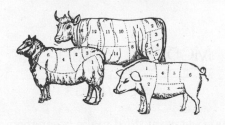

Mention meat for dinner and you're likely to get one of two responses. The uninformed will summon up sermons on cholesterol and fat, but those who know better are aware that healthful lean meat has made a comeback. Just take a look at meat in the market — there's more red and less of the fatty white. What's more, there are numerous cuts from which to choose, many of which are smaller and leaner than ever before.

Needless to say, if you try to cook these lean cuts using old cooking methods, you'll get tough, dry meat. But don't pour on the fat. We're about to give you great ideas for keeping meat loaf lean and moist and for marinating beef without any added fat. We'll also share lowfat cooking methods that keep lean pork, veal, and game meats succulent.

For a quick lowfat dinner, try Chinese Pork with Skinny Noodles. Or Jamaican Jerk Pork for a robust, low-calorie, no-salt-added meal. Thai Steak Salad and London Broil with Cognac and Mustard can both be made ahead and enjoyed warm or very slightly chilled. Whatever your choice, you'll prove to yourself that you don't have to give up meat to have a healthy diet.

Three Ways to Make Meat Loaf Leaner

- Buy lean meat, trim away visible fat, and grind it yourself in a meat grinder or food processor.
- Substitute cooked rice or barley for a third of the meat in your current meat loaf recipe. The grain cuts fat and adds fiber.
- Use two whites instead of one whole egg if your recipe calls for an egg.

MODERN MEAT LOAF

4 SERVINGS

Black bread and coarse mustard make great accompaniments.

1 pound lean ground beef
2 egg whites, lightly beaten
2 cloves garlic, mashed through a press
½ cup onion, peeled and finely chopped
1 carrot, grated
1 cup cooked rice
1 teaspoon thyme
½ teaspoon rosemary

Preheat the oven to 350°F.

In a large bowl combine all of the ingredients and mix well. (Using your hands is the easiest way.)

Spray an 8½ x 4½ x 3-inch loaf pan with nonstick vegetable spray and tip in the meat mixture. Pack it in well and smooth out the top with your hand. Bake until cooked through, about 50 minutes. (The meat will cook faster in glass or black metal pans.)

Let the loaf "relax" for about 10 minutes, then unmold and slice with a bread knife. Serve hot or slightly chilled.

Quick Oil-Free Marinades for Meats

For each marinade, combine the ingredients in a nonreactive dish and let the meat marinate for 1 to 2 hours. Then grill, broil, or roast.

- *Great with flank steak, sirloin, and top round:*
  1 bottle dark beer
  1 teaspoon coarse-type prepared mustard
  2 cloves garlic, mashed through a press
- *Perfect with pork:*
  ½ cup defatted beef stock
  ¼ cup dry white wine
  1 teaspoon oregano
  1 teaspoon celery seed
- *Excellent for venison and beef:*
  ½ cup red wine vinegar
  2 bay leaves, coarsely crushed
  2 cloves garlic, mashed through a press

Juicy Scoop

 For maximum juiciness without added fat, let cooked meats "relax" for about 10 minutes before slicing.

London Broil with Cognac and Mustard

4 SERVINGS

2 tablespoons cognac or brandy
2 tablespoons Worcestershire sauce
1 teaspoon dijon-style prepared mustard
¾ pound top round or flank steak, about 1-inch thick

In a small bowl combine the cognac, Worcestershire and mustard.

Set the meat in a shallow nonreactive dish and pour on the marinade. Be sure that the meat is completely coated. Marinate for an hour or two.

Prepare the grill or preheat the broiler. Set the meat on a raised rack over a drip pan and grill or broil about 5½ inches from the heat until cooked through the way you like it. About 5 minutes on each side will give you medium rare.

Let the meat "relax" for about 10 minutes, then slice thinly against the grain. Serve warm or slightly chilled.

Prime Cut

One way to cut fat and calories in stir fries and sautés is to reduce the amount of meat, replacing it with extra sliced vegetables. Instead of using a pound of meat for four persons, for instance, try cutting back to half or three-quarters of a pound and tossing in strips of colorful sweet peppers to make up the difference.

FAJITAS

4 SERVINGS

½ pound top round, trimmed of fat
  and sliced thinly against the grain
2 tablespoons freshly squeezed lemon juice
½ teaspoon freshly ground cumin
1 teaspoon oregano
2 cloves garlic, mashed through a press
½ teaspoon hot pepper sauce, or to taste
1 teaspoon brown sugar
2 teaspoons olive oil
1 onion, very thinly sliced
2 sweet peppers, cored and thinly sliced
  (you choose the colors)
4 soft flour tortillas
sliced fresh chilies and chopped ripe tomato for serving

In a nonreactive bowl combine the beef, lemon juice, cumin, oregano, garlic, hot pepper sauce, sugar, and oil. Marinate for about 30 minutes.

When you're ready to cook, heat a well-seasoned cast-iron skillet on medium-high. Add the onion and peppers and sizzle until limp, about 3 minutes. Then add the beef — marinade and all — and continue to sizzle until the beef has cooked through, about 4 minutes.

To serve, fill the tortillas with the beef mixture, chilies, and tomatoes.

THAI STEAK SALAD

4 SERVINGS

8 ounces lean sirloin or top round, about 1-inch thick
2 teaspoons reduced-sodium soy sauce
1 medium sweet onion, peeled and thinly sliced
1 medium cucumber, peeled and thinly sliced
1 tablespoon freshly squeezed lime juice
1 tablespoon Thai fish sauce (nam pla) or
  reduced-sodium soy sauce
½ teaspoon hot pepper sauce, or to taste
romaine leaves for serving

Preheat the broiler or prepare the grill. Sprinkle the sirloin with the 2 teaspoons of soy sauce and rub it into the surface. Broil or grill about 5½ inches from the heat source until cooked through the way you like it — about 7 minutes on each side for medium rare.

Let the steak "relax" for about 10 minutes, then slice thinly against the grain. Toss with the onion and cucumber.

In a small bowl combine the lime juice, Thai fish sauce, and hot pepper sauce. Pour over the salad and toss well to combine. Arrange the salad on romaine leaves and serve warm.

Pepper Power

Hot chilies can take a bite out of fat, calories and sodium in your cooking. One jalapeño, for instance, contains a mere 40 calories and contributes a snappy lowfat flavor to soups, sauces, stews, and condiments.

JAMAICAN JERK PORK

4 SERVINGS

¾ pound boneless pork loin
2 cloves garlic, mashed through a press
½ teaspoon hot sauce, or to taste
1 fresh hot chili pepper, minced (use gloves)
juice and pulp of 1 lime
pinch freshly ground nutmeg
1 tablespoon very finely minced fresh parsley
    or coriander (cilantro)
1 tablespoon peanut oil

Trim the pork of visible fat, then slice it into thin ribbons, against the grain.

Combine the garlic, hot pepper sauce, chili, lime juice, nutmeg, and parsley or coriander in a medium bowl and mix in the pork. Marinate for about 30 minutes.

Heat a nonstick sauté pan on medium heat, then add the oil. When the oil is warm, use a slotted spoon to transfer the pork from the marinade to the pan. Sauté until almost cooked through, about 4 minutes. Pour in the marinade and continue to sauté for another 30 seconds. Serve warm with rice and a cucumber salad.

Studies suggest that trimming the fat from meat before cooking gets rid of a few more calories and a bit more fat and cholesterol than trimming after cooking.

LOWER FAT RIBS
WITH GARLIC-TOMATO SAUCE

4 SERVINGS

2 pounds spareribs
boiling water
1 cup tomato sauce
4 cloves garlic, mashed through a press
1 teaspoon sage
freshly ground black pepper

Slice the slabs into individual ribs, trim off visible fat, and add the ribs to a large pot of boiling water. Continue to boil for about 7 minutes. (This process will help rid the ribs of excess fat.) Keep an eye on the pot to avoid boilovers.

Preheat the oven to 400°F. Drain the ribs and pat them dry. Then spray a roasting pan with nonstick vegetable spray and arrange the ribs in it.

Combine the tomato sauce, garlic, sage, and pepper in a medium bowl and paint each rib with the mixture. Roast the ribs until cooked through, about 30 minutes, basting occasionally. Serve hot.

Pig Out

In the last few years we've been hearing that pork has become leaner. How can this be? Two reasons: First, there's less fat in the feed; second, the animals are brought to slaughter at a younger age, before they have time to fatten up. To enjoy this new lean pork with moist and juicy results (and without adding fat), cook it for slightly less time at a lower temperature. You can tell strips are done when their juices run clear. Roasts should have an internal temperature of at least 160°F.

CHINESE PORK WITH SKINNY NOODLES

4 SERVINGS

½ pound lean pork, sliced thinly against the grain
2 cloves garlic, mashed through a press
1 teaspoon reduced-sodium soy sauce
2 teaspoons peanut oil
1 cup sliced mushrooms
1 onion, peeled and very thinly sliced
1½ cups cooked vermicelli
⅔ cup defatted beef stock
2 scallions, very finely minced, for garnish

Combine the pork, garlic, and soy sauce in a medium bowl and marinate for about 30 minutes.

When you're ready, heat a wok or nonstick sauté pan on high, then pour in the oil. Toss in the mushrooms and onion and stir-fry until fragrant and beginning to brown, about 2½ minutes. Add the pork — marinade and all — and continue to stir-fry until cooked through, about 2½ more minutes.

Use a slotted spoon to remove the vegetables and pork from the wok and toss them with the vermicelli. Then pour the stock into the wok and boil until fragrant and reduced by half, about 3 minutes. Pour over the pork and vermicelli and toss well. Garnish with the scallions and serve warm.

Name Your Game

Game meats such as venison and buffalo can make lean and delicious eating. The meat does, however, vary in flavor and nutrition depending on the type of animal and its diet. Wild whitetail deer, for instance, eat leaves and weeds and can taste gamey and unpleasant. The secret is to buy ranch-raised game which feed on grass and are consistently tender, tasty, and healthful. An average 3-ounce serving of venison contains about 115 calories and just over 1 gram of fat. Bite for bite, that's one-third the calories of beef and one-eighth the fat.

Substitute venison for beef in chili, stew, curries, meat loaf, soup, or kabobs, but shorten the cooking time a bit, since the meat is leaner. For a moist venison roast without added fat, seal it in an oven cooking bag before roasting. Types of venison to look for are axis, blackbuck antelope, nilgai antelope, and sika. If you can't locate them in your area, write to the Texas Wild Game Cooperative, P.O. Box 530, Ingram, Texas 78025.

Buffalo is beautiful deep-red meat that contains a mere 159 calories per 100 grams (about ¼ pound) serving, with 5.4 grams of fat. Like venison, it can be substituted for beef in many dishes. To keep this lean meat moist without adding fat, use moist cooking methods such as braising or gentle stewing. When roasting, lower the oven temperature by 25 to 50 degrees and check for doneness sooner than you would with beef. There are over 500 buffalo ranches in the United States, but if you can't find buffalo in your area write to the National Buffalo Association, P.O. Box 565, Ft. Pierre, South Dakota 57532.

On the Lamb

For extra leanness, buy lamb from New Zealand or Australia. Unlike U.S. lamb, the down-under type is never fattened with grain before marketing. But regardless of where your lamb grazes, be sure to trim away visible fat before cooking.

GRILLED LEG OF LAMB
WITH ROSEMARY, GARLIC, AND CURRANTS

16 SERVINGS

1 leg (approximately 7½ pounds) of lamb,
*   boned and butterflied*
2 teaspoons rosemary
¼ cup currants, minced
4 cloves garlic, mashed through a press
1 tablespoon prepared dijon-style mustard
1 cup plain lowfat yogurt

Use a sharp knife to trim the visible fat from the lamb. You'll come across what's called the silver, or fell—it's sort of like a very hard fat and should be cut away at this point because it's nearly impossible to remove when the lamb is cooked. Set the lamb in a large nonreactive baking dish.

Combine the rosemary, currants, garlic, mustard, and yogurt in a medium bowl. Spread over the lamb and rub it in well. Cover and refrigerate for up to 2 days.

When you're ready, prepare the grill or preheat the broiler. Set the lamb on a rack about 5½ inches from the heat source and broil until cooked through the way you like it, about 10 minutes on each side for medium rare. You'll need some strong tongs and a spatula to flip the lamb, it's heavy. Let the lamb "relax" for about 10 minutes before slicing thinly against the grain. Serve warm or very slightly chilled.

LAMB CHOPS WITH CURRY BUTTER

4 SERVINGS

Great with a salad of chopped cabbage and apples or with a side dish of sautéed apples.

> 1 tablespoon sweet butter or margarine
> 1 teaspoon good quality curry powder
> 8 lean rib lamb chops, about 3 ounces each,
>   trimmed of visible fat

Melt the butter in a large nonstick sauté pan, then sprinkle in the curry powder.

Set the chops in the pan and sauté until the chops are cooked through the way you like them, 3 to 4 minutes on each side for medium rare. Serve warm.

Note: If your pan's not big enough, prepare this recipe in 2 batches.

Try a Little Tenderness

Veal can dry out easily during cooking, which is why many cooks pour on the cream sauce. But you can keep veal tender without the heavy cream. Veal scallops (thin slices) should be cooked quickly over medium-high heat until pink inside. Don't overcook. For veal stew, adding cold water (instead of hot) to the meat, then bringing to a boil, will help keep it tender. And for roasts, pot-style cooking with lots of liquid is best.

VEAL SCALLOPS WITH MUSTARD SAUCE

4 SERVINGS

¾ *veal scallops*
2 *tablespoons flour (you may not need it all)*
1 *teaspoon olive oil*
3 *tablespoons dry sherry*
3 *tablespoons chicken stock*
1 *tablespoon prepared dijon-style mustard*

The veal scallops should be of even thickness. If they're not, arrange the pieces between 2 sheets of waxed paper and flatten by smacking with the back of a heavy pan. Then sprinkle on the flour.

Heat a large nonstick pan on medium high and add the oil. Set in the veal and sizzle until cooked through, about 1½ minutes on each side. Don't overcook. Remove the veal from the pan and keep it warm.

Add the sherry, stock, and mustard to the pan and bring to a boil, whisking constantly. When the sauce has reduced by half, drizzle it over the veal and serve warm.

VEAL CHOPS WITH FRESH BASIL SAUCE

4 SERVINGS

4 veal loin chops, about ½ pound each
2 tablespoons flour (you may not need it all)
1 teaspoon olive oil
1 teaspoon sweet butter or margarine
⅓ cup minced fresh basil
½ cup dry white wine
1 teaspoon prepared coarse-style mustard

Sprinkle the chops with the flour. Then heat a large nonstick sauté pan on medium-high. Add the oil and butter, and when the butter has melted, set in the chops. Sizzle until cooked through, about 3 to 4 minutes on each side. Remove the chops from the pan and keep them warm.

Add the basil, wine, and mustard to the oil and butter in the pan and bring it to a boil, whisking frequently. Continue to boil until thickened, about 1 minute. Pour the sauce over the chops and serve warm.

Pasta and Vegetable Entrées

If you're one of those people who thinks that vegetarian food is brown and boring, we're about to change your mind. Many people who have switched to a diet high in vegetables and grains to eat leaner and reduce the odds of heart disease and cancer, have found to their surprise that it is a delicious and satisfying way to eat.

Take pasta, for example. A one-cup serving has a moderate 200 calories. We'll show you how to liven it up with flavorful fresh vegetables and lowfat cheeses that keep the calorie count very reasonable. Try Angel Hair with Mushroom Sauce or Linguini with Green Chilies and Pine Nuts. You'll even learn how to make a luscious yet lean lasagne. In a hurry? Check our chart on Quick and Healthy Tosses for Pasta.

If you like our pastas, you'll love our Skinny Pizza. We'll show you how to create a crisp, high-fiber crust plus a variety of tasty toppings. If your family is likely to be suspicious of vegetable entrées, there isn't a better way to introduce them to the delicious possibilities.

From there, treat them to our no-fat-added risotto, savory pies made with our lowfat crust, and our tender eggplant made without the deep-fryer. For company, we recommend our rich-tasting soufflé that's light on fat, and for a quick diet dish, our Chinese rice needs no frying.

Before you know it, Vegetarian Night might be the most popular one of all in your household.

Pasta-bilities

Pairing the right sauce with the right pasta is an important culinary decision. The right combination of textures and colors can keep you so satisfied that you won't even think about reaching for fatty sauces.

A good rule is that delicate pastas go with delicate sauces and thicker pastas pair up with thicker sauces. Here are some other suggestions:

- *Small whole wheat shells:* Adorn with minced fresh basil or rosemary, freshly grated Romano cheese, and a splash of olive oil.
- *Small white shells:* Toss with steamed green beans and pesto; serve warm or very slightly chilled.
- *Medium shells* (whole wheat and white): Enrich with tomato sauce with mushrooms; serve warm. Or serve as a salad with herbed lowfat yogurt.
- *Large shells:* Stuff with minced chilies, corn kernels, and lowfat cheddar; then bake until the cheese melts.
- *Rotini:* Combine warm tomato and spinach rotini with crumbled blue cheese and marjoram. Try white rotini with sweet red pepper puree. Fuselli will work with these sauces too.
- *Fettuccini:* Toss with blanched Chinese peas, toasted sesame oil, and mashed roasted garlic.
- *Rigatoni and mostaccioli:* Stir-fry big slices of sweet onions and colorful peppers. Toss with pasta and serve warm.
- *Flavored pastas:* These include lemon-pepper, tomato-basil, wild mushroom, and Cajun. Sprinkle with freshly grated parmesan, a splash of olive oil, and a twist of black pepper. That's all they need.

Four Ways to Make Lasagne Leaner

- Use part-skim ricotta instead of whole-milk ricotta
- Substitute chopped vegetables for some or all of the meat
- Use lean ground turkey instead of ground beef
- In place of whole-milk mozzarella, use part-skim mozzarella or soy mozzarella

LITE LASAGNE

4 SERVINGS

4 cooked lasagne noodles
(whole wheat or spinach varieties are nice)
½ cup part-skim ricotta
½ cup finely chopped broccoli, blanched for about 1 minute
½ cup finely minced raw fresh spinach
2 scallions, very finely minced
½ cup tomato sauce
4 teaspoons part-skim mozzarella

Preheat the oven to 375°F.

Pat the noodles dry, then lay them out on the counter.

In a medium bowl fold together the riccota, broccoli, spinach, and scallions. Divide this mixture evenly between the noodles, spreading it out with the back of a spoon.

Roll up the noodles as you would a jelly roll, then set them in a baking dish that's been sprayed with nonstick vegetable spray. (At this point you can stop and refrigerate the lasagne until you're ready.) Pour on the tomato sauce, sprinkle on the cheese, and bake until cooked through and the cheese has melted, about 20 minutes. Serve warm.

Down the Drain with Salt

 Rinsing olives in water and vinegar before using will rid them of some of their surface salt.

SPAGHETTI TORTE WITH OLIVES AND FETA

4 TO 6 SERVINGS

1 clove garlic, mashed through a press
3 tablespoons chopped green olives
2 tablespoons crumbled feta cheese
2 scallions, very finely minced
3 cups cooked spaghetti
1 egg, beaten
2 egg whites, beaten
1 tablespoon olive oil
chopped fresh tomatoes for serving

In a large bowl combine the garlic, cloves, feta, scallions, spaghetti, egg, and egg whites. Use your hands to toss the ingredients, making sure everything is well combined.

Heat the oil on medium in a 10-inch nonstick pan and when it's warm add the spaghetti mixture. Quickly flatten it out to form a pancake, then weight it down with a flat plate. Let it cook until it's beginning to brown, about 3 to 3½ minutes. Then use the plate and a spatula to flip it over. Continue to cook (plate on top) until the second side is beginning to brown and the torte is firm, about 3 more minutes. Cut into wedges with a knife or kitchen shears and serve warm with the chopped tomatoes.

A Toast to Nuts

Although nuts are high in calories, adding just a few won't push the calorie count objectionably high and will make for rich flavor. The secret is to toast them first, which brings out their robust flavors so that smaller amounts suffice.

LINGUINI WITH GREEN CHILIES AND TOASTED PINE NUTS

4 SERVINGS

This unusual recipe is also delicious served at room temperature as a salad.

2 tablespoons pine nuts
2 teaspoons olive oil
2 cloves garlic, peeled and thinly sliced
2 mild green chilies, cored and finely chopped
3 ripe tomatoes, cored, juiced, and chopped
2 cups cooked linguini
freshly grated parmesan for sprinkling

Heat a large nonstick sauté pan on medium-high, then toss in the nuts. Sauté them until toasty brown, about 2 minutes. (Take care that they don't burn.) Remove the nuts and keep them handy.

With the pan still warm, add the olive oil. When the oil is warm, add the garlic, chilies, and tomatoes and sauté until the vegetables are beginning to wilt, about 3 minutes. Immediately toss with the linguini and pine nuts, sprinkle with the parmesan, and serve warm.

Five Quick and Healthy Pasta Tosses

Make pasta ahead, toss with a bit of olive oil, cover, and refrigerate. When you're ready, toss with:

- Sautéed broccoli, minced garlic, and toasted sunflower seeds
- Steamed zucchini and yellow squash, minced fresh basil, and chopped ripe tomato
- Sautéed mushrooms, garden peas, and part-skim ricotta
- Steamed julienned beets and carrots, crumbled rosemary, and a splash of olive oil
- Part-skim ricotta, minced fresh dill, and minced fresh chives

Cutting Cholesterol

Cooking with olive oil and other monounsaturated oils can help lower harmful levels of cholesterol. Luckily, olive oil is a perfect taste partner with naturally lowfat pasta!

Say "Good-bye" to Salt

Instead of salting the cooking water for pasta, toss in dried herbs. Try rosemary, basil, or thyme. They add flavor without the sodium.

TINY PASTA, MOROCCAN-STYLE

4 SERVINGS

Accompany this tasty dish with orange sections and a salad of interesting greens.

1 tablespoon olive oil
1 large onion, peeled and chopped
1 large tomato, cored, seeded, and chopped
2 tablespoons raisins
½ cup cooked chick peas
½ teaspoon cinnamon
½ teaspoon saffron threads, crushed
2 cups cooked couscous, or other very tiny pasta
    (even orzo will do)
⅓ cup chopped fresh parsley

Heat a nonstick pan on medium, then pour in the oil. When it's warm, add the onion and sauté until medium-browned, about 8 minutes.

Add the tomato, raisins, chick peas, cinnamon, and saffron and continue to cook until the tomato is wilted and the sauce is fragrant, about 5 minutes.

Combine the couscous, parsley, and tomato mixture in a large bowl, tossing well to combine but taking care not to crush the couscous. Serve warm.

Always buy parmesan (and other cheeses for grating) in small blocks and grate them yourself. The flavor of fresh cheese is more robust so you can add less. And that means that you add less sodium than if you use the less flavorful packaged varieties.

FETTUCCINI WITH KALE

4 SERVINGS

2 teaspoons olive oil
2 cloves garlic, peeled and thinly sliced
2 cups finely shredded kale
⅔ cup chicken stock
2 cups cooked fettuccini
freshly grated parmesan for sprinkling

Heat a large nonstick sauté pan on medium, then pour in the oil. When it's warm, add the garlic and sauté until just fragrant, about 1 minute.

Next, add the kale and continue to sauté for several more minutes. Then pour in the stock, cover loosely, and raise the heat to medium-high. Let the sauce bubble until the kale is just tender, about 2½ minutes. Then toss with the fettuccini, sprinkle with the parmesan, and serve warm in shallow bowls.

Variation: Substitute spinach or broccoli rabe for the kale.

Mushrooms for Meat

Chopped sautéed fresh mushrooms are a great substitute for ground meat in pasta sauces. They add texture and flavor without adding the fat or calories found in ground meat. In fact, a Finnish company has discovered this secret and is using wild mushrooms to lower the fat content of its sausage.

ANGEL HAIR WITH MUSHROOM SAUCE

4 SERVINGS

Great with a salad of mixed spring greens.

2 teaspoons olive oil or sweet butter
½ cup chopped fresh button mushrooms
½ cup chopped fresh shiitake mushrooms
2 shallots, peeled and minced
1 teaspoon basil
½ teaspoon thyme
splash hot pepper sauce, or to taste
⅔ cup chicken stock
2 tablespoons dry white wine
2 cups cooked angel hair pasta

Heat a large nonstick sauté pan on medium, then add the olive oil. When it's warm (or when the butter has melted) add the mushrooms, shallots, basil, and thyme; sauté until the mushrooms have darkened and softened, about 3 minutes.

Add the hot pepper sauce, stock, and wine to the mushroom mixture in the pan and increase the heat to high. Let the sauce bubble, uncovered, until the liquid has reduced by about a third. Toss with the angel hair and serve warm.

Out of the Salad into the Sauce

Lowfat salad dressings aren't just for salads, you know. They can also make great light sauces for pasta. Try a lowfat yogurt-based dressing with rotini or fuselli, a reduced-calorie herbed mayonnaise with whole wheat elbows, and an herbed vinaigrette with spinach fettuccini. Fast and fabulous.

SKINNY NOODLES WITH SESAME VINAIGRETTE

4 SERVINGS

2 teaspoons regular or reduced-sodium soy sauce
1 tablespoon rice vinegar or other mild white vinegar
2 teaspoons toasted sesame oil
½ teaspoon fresh ginger, peeled and very finely minced
1 clove garlic, mashed through a press
2 scallions, very finely minced
1 tablespoon sesame seeds
2 cups cooked skinny pasta, such as vermicelli
    or buckwheat soba

In a large bowl whisk together the soy sauce, vinegar, oil, ginger, and garlic. Add the scallions, sesame seeds, and pasta; toss well to combine. Serve room temperature or very slightly chilled.

Vegetable Variations

If colors and textures are thoughtfully chosen, a simple sauté or stir-fry of vegetables can be a lowfat yet exciting sauce for pasta. Julienne of carrot, yellow squash, and leek, plus a pinch of tarragon, are wonderful with linguini.

SPAGHETTI WITH STIR-FRIED VEGETABLES

4 SERVINGS

2 teaspoons olive oil
2 shallots, peeled and thinly sliced
1 sweet red or yellow pepper, cored and sliced
1 green bell pepper, cored and sliced
½ cup broccoli, chopped
½ teaspoon thyme
½ teaspoon oregano
2 cups cooked spaghetti
freshly grated parmesan for sprinkling

Heat a wok on high, then pour in the oil. When it's warm, add the shallots, peppers, broccoli, thyme, and oregano and stir-fry until the vegetables are just tender, about 3 to 4 minutes.

Toss with the spaghetti and parmesan; serve warm.

Fresh or Canned?

When preparing a lowfat, low-salt tomato sauce, the flavor of the tomatoes is all-important. It's a simple fact: If the tomatoes are bland, the sauce will be, too. So even though fresh produce is generally the best, when you can't find rich, ripe fresh tomatoes, use canned instead. Many brands are no-salt-added, so check labels.

RIGATONI WITH FRESH TOMATO SAUCE AND BLUE CHEESE

4 SERVINGS

2 teaspoons olive oil
2 tablespoons minced onion
1 clove garlic, mashed through a press
1 pound rich, ripe tomatoes, cored, seeded, and chopped
2 teaspoons balsamic vinegar, or other robust vinegar
2 cups cooked rigatoni
2 tablespoons crumbled blue cheese

Heat a large nonstick sauté pan on medium and pour in the oil. When it's warm, add the onion and garlic and sauté until fragrant and barely wilted, about 2 minutes.

Slide in the tomatoes (juice, too) and the vinegar and bring the sauce to a boil. Continue to boil until the sauce has thickened, about 4 minutes, stirring occasionally.

Toss the sauce with the rigatoni and blue cheese and serve warm.

SPAGHETTI SQUASH
WITH CREAMY SPINACH SAUCE

4 SERVINGS

Delicious with a side dish of tomatoes and fresh basil.

> 1 spaghetti squash (about 3 pounds)
> 1 cup spinach leaves, washed well and patted dry
>   on paper towels
> 1/3 cup buttermilk
> 2 scallions, chopped
> freshly grated parmesan for sprinkling

Preheat the oven to 425°F.

Halve the squash lengthwise and set the halves cut side down in a roasting pan. Pour in about an inch of water and bake until the halves are tender, 25 to 30 minutes.

Meanwhile, combine the spinach, buttermilk, and scallions in a processor or blender and whiz until smooth.

When the squash is ready, remove the seeds and use a dinner fork to fluff out the spaghetti strands. Immediately toss with the parmesan and sauce and serve warm.

Pizza Panache

Yes, you can have your pizza and eat healthfully too. Just make it yourself, following the guidelines that are most relevant to your health:

- For extra fiber, use part or all whole wheat flour
- To cut calories, roll the dough super thin
- Use low-calorie, lowfat toppings, such as sliced fresh vegetables, instead of sausage or meat
- Slash sodium by using crushed tomatoes instead of salty tomato sauce

• Omit excess fat by using part-skim cheeses and by halving the amount of cheese used

SKINNY PIZZA

4 SERVINGS

1 package active dry yeast
1 teaspoon sugar
¾ cup lukewarm water
2 teaspoons olive oil
1¼ cups unbleached flour
1¼ cups whole wheat bread flour
½ teaspoon salt
⅔ cup crushed tomatoes
¼ cup freshly shredded part-skim mozzarella or parmesan

In a large bowl mix together the yeast, sugar, water, and oil. Add in the flours and salt and use your hands to mix until the dough forms a shape.

Turn the dough onto a floured counter and knead for about 10 minutes. Then set it into a lightly oiled bowl, cover with plastic wrap, and let rise until double in size, about 35 minutes.

Punch the dough down and let it rise again for about 20 minutes.

Preheat the oven to 500°F.

Roll the dough out to a 13-inch circle, then set it on a lightly oiled perforated pizza pan. Crimp up the edges and bake blind — without filling — for about 10 minutes. Spread on the tomatoes, sprinkle on the cheese, and bake for about 7 minutes more.

Cut into wedges and serve warm.

Ideas for Lean Pizza Toppings

• Stir-fried vegetables
• Poached shrimp or chicken
• Blanched mushrooms and sweet pepper slices
• Slivered sweet onions

Herb Wisdom

🍴 Sage adds a robust, meaty flavor to foods without adding fat or calories. Try it with omelettes and crepes.

Cut the Crust

🍴 The dietary downfall of many pies, tarts, and quiches is their fatty crusts. What to do? Simply omit the crust and bake as usual. A great time-saver, too.

BAKED ONION TART

4 TO 6 SERVINGS

Perfect with vegetable soup.

1 tablespoon olive oil
2 large sweet onions, peeled, sliced, and separated into rings
2 cloves garlic, mashed through a press
2 shallots, peeled and minced
2 tablespoons minced fresh chives
1 cup skim or whole milk
1 egg
2 egg whites
1 teaspoon sage

Preheat the oven to 375°F.

Heat a well-seasoned 10-inch cast-iron skillet on medium-high and pour in the oil. When it's warm, add the onions, garlic, shallots, and chives, and sauté until the onions are just soft, about 3 minutes.

In a medium bowl whisk together the milk, egg, and whites. Rub the sage between your hands to release its flavor, then whisk it in, too.

Pour the egg mixture over the onions and bake until set, about 30 minutes. Slice into wedges; serve warm.

When the Crust Is a Must

Cut calories by replacing the traditional fat-packed crust with one made from cooked rice or potatoes. Our easy Savory Rice Crust shows you how. Try it with quiche or meat pies.

SAVORY RICE CRUST

MAKES 1 CRUST, ENOUGH FOR 8 SERVINGS

2½ cups cooked rice (medium-grain brown works well)
1 tablespoon sweet butter or margarine, melted
1 egg, beaten
1 tablespoon unbleached flour

Preheat the oven to 350°F.

Spray a 9-inch glass pie dish with nonstick vegetable spray and add the rice.

In a small bowl whisk together the butter, egg, and flour. Pour the mixture over the rice and pat into a crust, firmly pressing against the pan edges and bottom.

Bake until set, about 20 minutes. Then, to seal the crust, broil it until it feels dry, about 1½ minutes. To use, scoop in a filling and bake until set.

Variation: Substitute 2½ cups of diced steamed potatoes for the rice. Be sure to pat them dry before using.

Why Fry?

Many foods that are traditionally fried are even more delicious when baked. Fritters, savory pancakes, and croquettes are good examples. For best results, be sure the oven is hot enough, about 400° to 425°F. Keep an eye on the food, however, so it doesn't burn.

CHINESE OMELETTE
(EGG FOO YONG)

4 TO 6 SERVINGS

1 cup large fresh bean sprouts
3 scallions, minced
2 carrots, grated
1 sweet red pepper, cored and minced
1 egg
3 egg whites
2 teaspoons soy sauce, regular or reduced-sodium
toasted sesame oil for serving

Preheat the oven to 400°F.

Spray a 9-inch glass pie dish with nonstick vegetable spray. Then add the sprouts, scallions, carrots, and peppers.

In a medium bowl whisk together the egg, egg whites, and soy sauce. Pour the egg mixture over the vegetables and bake until set, about 15 minutes. Cut into wedges with kitchen shears; sprinkle with the sesame oil before serving warm.

Get into the Blend

Instead of buying the same old rice, try some of the many interesting rice blends that are available at supermarkets. They usually contain a mixture of medium-grain brown rice—a source of fiber—plus one or two aromatic rices for flavor without added fat.

(UN)FRIED RICE, CHINESE STYLE

4 SERVINGS

Great stuffed in cooked halved winter squash.

2 teaspoons peanut oil or canola oil
1 medium onion, peeled, sliced, and separated into rings
2 cloves garlic, mashed through a press
1 cup chopped broccoli
1 cup shredded spinach leaves
2 cups cooked rice (medium-grain brown or a blend)

Heat a large nonstick pan or wok on medium-high and pour in the oil. When it's warm, add the onion and sauté until beginning to wilt, about 3 minutes. Then add the garlic, broccoli, and spinach, and continue to sauté until fragrant and just tender, about 3 minutes more. Stir in the rice, heat through, and serve warm.

Zap More Fat

🍴 As you may know, risotto is a wonderfully creamy rice that contains no cream at all. But to cook risotto on the stovetop or in the oven, you need to add some fat to keep the rice from sticking to the pan. Solution? Cook the rice in your microwave to keep it fat-free.

RISOTTO WITH TINY WHITE BEANS AND PEAS

4 SERVINGS

Delicious with steamed artichokes and marinated mushrooms.

1 cup arborio rice, uncooked
3 cups hot chicken or vegetable stock
⅔ cup cooked tiny white beans (canned and rinsed are fine)
⅔ cup garden peas (if using frozen, don't defrost)
1 leek, washed well, trimmed and minced
1 bay leaf
2 to 3 tablespoons freshly grated parmesan cheese

Combine the rice, stock, beans, peas, leek, and bay leaf in a microwave ring pan. Microwave, uncovered, on full power until most of the stock has been absorbed, about 16 minutes. Be sure to stop and stir midway.

Let stand for about 8 minutes, stirring occasionally. Then fold in the cheese and serve warm.

Variation: Use crumbled feta cheese or mild chevre instead of the parmesan.

Tempting Tempeh

Famous in Indonesian cuisines, tempeh is a savory cake made of beans and grains. Soy is the best-known tempeh ingredient, but barley, brown rice, millet, and quinoa are also popular. Although made from vegetable foods only, tempeh has a pleasant, winey taste and a substantial, meaty texture. Unlike meats, however, tempeh is cholesterol-free and high in fiber. Look for it in the freezer cases of natural food stores and many supermarkets. In addition to using it in tempeh dishes, add small amounts of it to stir-fries, soups, and stews to vary their flavor and texture.

TEMPEH WITH FRESH VEGETABLES AND HERBS

4 SERVINGS

2 teaspoons olive oil
10 ounces tempeh, cut into 1-inch chunks
1 sweet pepper, cored and chunked
1 medium onion, peeled and chopped
1 medium (about 6 ounces) zucchini, chunked but not peeled
1 clove garlic, mashed through a press
3 tablespoons finely minced fresh basil
2 medium tomatoes, chopped

Heat a well-seasoned cast-iron skillet on medium, then pour in the oil. (If you don't have cast-iron, use a nonstick sauté pan). When it's warm, toss in the tempeh and sauté until lightly browned, about 5 minutes.

Add the pepper, onion, zucchini, garlic, and basil, and continue to sauté until the vegetables are fragrant and just tender, about 5 minutes.

Tip in the tomatoes and raise the heat to high; heat through. Serve warm.

CORN AND SWEET PEPPER SOUFFLÉ

½ cup fresh or frozen sweet corn kernels
¾ cup skim milk
2 tablespoons sweet butter or margarine
2 tablespoons unbleached flour
1 sweet red pepper cored and finely chopped
¼ cup part-skim ricotta
2 eggs, separated
2 additional egg whites
freshly grated parmesan for dusting

Preheat the oven to 450°F.

Meanwhile, tip the corn and milk into a processor or blender and whiz until smooth. Set aside.

Melt the butter in a large nonstick sauté pan. Sprinkle in the flour and whisk over low heat for about a minute. Add the corn mixture and sweet pepper; simmer until slightly thickened. Add the ricotta and continue to cook for about 2 minutes more. Remove from the heat and let cool a bit. Then whisk in the egg yolks.

Using a hand mixer, beat the 4 egg whites until they form stiff peaks. Then fold in a scoop of the corn mixture. Carefully fold the whites mixture back into the remaining corn mixture.

Dust the inside of a 1½-quart soufflé dish with the parmesan. Scoop in the corn mixture. Set the soufflé dish on the center rack in the oven and reduce the heat to 350°F. Bake until puffed, about 30 minutes. (Remember not to open the oven for spotchecks, or the soufflé will fall.) Serve immediately. Steamed broccoli makes a superb accompaniment.

Exceptional Eggplant

One way to tenderize eggplant without deep-frying is to broil it. Simply slash sliced eggplant with a surface "X" on one side and broil for about 5 minutes on each side. If the eggplant is dry, rub the slices with olive oil before broiling. Use the broiled slices in eggplant parmesan or in casseroles.

MOUSSAKA MINUS MEAT

4 TO 6 SERVINGS

1 pound eggplant
1 tablespoon olive oil
1 medium onion, peeled and chopped
2 cloves garlic, peeled and chopped
1½ cups tomato sauce
1 teaspoon oregano
1 egg
1 egg white, beaten
2 tablespoons freshly grated parmesan
1 cup part-skim ricotta
½ teaspoon freshly grated nutmeg

Preheat the broiler. Starting at the short end, cut the eggplant into ½-inch-thick slices and arrange them in a single layer on a cookie sheet. Rub both sides of each round with a bit of olive oil, then use a knife to slash an "X" on the top of each slice. Broil until tender, about 5 minutes on each side. Remove the eggplant from the oven and set aside.

Lower oven to 375°F.

Heat a nonstick sauté pan on medium. When it's warm, pour in the rest of the oil. Add the onion and garlic and sauté until just tender, about 4 minutes. Then add the tomato sauce and oregano; stir to combine. Remove the pan from the heat and set aside also.

In a medium bowl whisk together the egg, egg white, parmesan, ricotta, and nutmeg. Then set it aside, along with the eggplant and tomato sauce.

Spray a 2-quart casserole dish with nonstick vegetable spray. Pour in half of the tomato sauce. Next, layer on half the eggplant slices and cover with all the cheese mixture. Layer on the remaining eggplant slices and top with the remaining sauce. Cover and bake until cooked through, about 40 minutes. Serve warm.

Appetizers, Snacks, and Beverages

A pantry filled with fatty snacks and sugary sodas can sabotage an otherwise healthy diet. A sad but true example is the man who feels he can splurge on a cream pie because he had oat bran for breakfast.

The best way to forget about empty-calorie snacks is simply not to buy them. Instead, pick up the ingredients for our lowfat dips and crackers; preparing them takes only a little more effort than opening a package of a convenient but unhealthful ready-to-eat prepared snack. Fill your kitchen with the snack foods recommended in this chapter and you'll be ready when an attack of the munchies strikes.

Enjoy our appetizers as starters for meals, or combine several for a casual dinner. Spread our Salmon and Caper Pâté on our homemade Crostini, for instance, and serve with a lively vegetable platter to make a mouth-watering summer dinner. Accompany this with a sparkling cider or any one of our reduced-sugar, salt-free beverages.

The Calcium Connection

The tiny bones in canned fish such as salmon and sardines contain valuable amounts of calcium — without the saturated fat of whole-milk dairy products. These tasty fish enhance antipastos, appetizer salads, and cheese trays.

SALMON AND CAPER PÂTÉ

MAKES ABOUT 1¹/₃ CUPS

Serve with crusty bread, whole grain crackers, or cucumber rounds.

1 can (7¾ ounces) salmon
¼ cup lowfat cottage cheese
2 tablespoons reduced-fat cream cheese
1½ tablespoons very finely minced onion
1 tablespoon very finely minced fresh parsley
2 teaspoons very finely minced capers

Drain the salmon, then remove and discard any skin and large bones.

In a small bowl combine the salmon and cottage cheese. Work in the cream cheese, onion, parsley, and capers with a fork until the mixture is spreadable.

Variation: Substitute drained sardines for the salmon.

No Vampires

Even if you're not a garlic lover, we guarantee you'll love roasted garlic. Its texture is soft and creamy and its taste amazingly mild. Prove it to yourself. Just spread some on a crusty loaf and you'll think you're savoring buttery garlic bread. Only your waistline will know that there's no butter added.

ROASTED GARLIC

MAKES 1 BULB

Roasted garlic is also delicious when squeezed from its peel and tossed with roasted sweet peppers, page 84. Or puree the roasted and peeled garlic in a processor along with some part-skim ricotta and enjoy as a dip for fresh vegetables.

1 whole bulb garlic, unpeeled
1 tablespoon olive oil

Preheat the oven to 450°F.

Separate the bulb into cloves and put them in a small baking dish. Don't peel. Pour on the olive oil and toss well.

Roast until the cloves are soft and tender, about 25 minutes. Stir occasionally to prevent burning.

To serve, squeeze the garlic meat out of its papery peel onto a hunk of warm, crusty bread. Spread and enjoy.

GRILLED MUSHROOM BROCHETTES

4 SERVINGS

*1 pound large mushrooms (about 2 inches in diameter),
    stems removed*
boiling water for blanching
1 teaspoon reduced-sodium soy sauce
2 teaspoons Worcestershire sauce
2 tablespoons chili sauce or ketchup
2 cloves garlic, mashed through a press

Blanch the mushrooms in the boiling water for 3 minutes.
Then drain and pat dry.

In a 9-inch glass pie dish combine the soy sauce, Worcestershire, chili sauce or ketchup, and garlic. Toss in the mushrooms
and marinate for about an hour.

Preheat the broiler or prepare the grill. Then thread the
mushrooms through their sides with thin, flat skewers.

Set the skewers on a rack 5½ inches from the heat source and
broil or grill until burnished, about 4 minutes on each side. Serve
warm.

Reduced-Fat Cheeses

When thinking of lowfat snacks, cheese rarely comes to mind.
Let's face it, a plate of brie — with 80% butterfat — is not in the
program if you want to stay lean and healthy. Fortunately,
cheese makers have been creating new reduced-fat varieties that
don't taste a bit like diet food. You may be acquainted with
lowfat cottage cheese and part-skim ricotta, but here are some
additions to the list:

• *Sapsago:* Made from buttermilk, skim milk, and herbs, this is
   a strong-tasting grating cheese. For a lowfat cheese bread,
   grate sapsago on rounds of French-type bread and broil until
   golden. Serve warm.

- *Soy cheese:* Not to be confused with tofu, soy cheeses are available in mozzarella and cheddar styles and actually melt when heated. They are cholesterol-free and low in fat—a big plus. Try the mozzarella atop a pizza.
- *Gammelost:* This is a crumbly blue-veined type from Norway that's made from skim milk. It's quite aromatic and makes a delicious stuffing in hollowed-out cherry tomatoes.
- *Baker's cheese and pot cheese:* Mild-tasting and soft, these cheeses are great stand-ins for fattening cream cheese. Baker's cheese is a bit sharper than pot, but both are great for dips. Or fold in a bit of minced fresh dill and spread on zucchini rounds.

Two Easy Lowfat Cheeses to Make Yourself

- *Yogurt Cheese:* Line a strainer with a double thickness of paper towels and set it in the sink. Scoop in 4 cups nonfat yogurt and let drain overnight. If you must put the draining cheese in the refrigerator, set the strainer in a large bowl to catch the liquid as it drips. After draining, you'll have 1½ cups of thick and delicious cheese to use in spreads or dips. Store refrigerated for up to a week.
- *Buttermilk cheese:* Pour 2 cups lowfat buttermilk in a medium saucepan and heat on medium. Watch carefully and you'll see the wrinkly buttermilk curds move away from the sides of the pan to the middle. When the milk starts to simmer around the edges, remove from the heat. This will take 4 to 5 minutes. Don't boil. Cover loosely with a paper towel and let cool for 2 to 3 hours. Don't stir or disturb. Line a strainer with a single thickness of paper towel and strain the cheese over the sink, discarding the liquidy part. You'll have about ⅔ cup of creamy cheese to use in spreads or as a lowfat filling for crepes and omelettes. Stir and store refrigerated for up to a week.

Veggies at Their Best

It's almost impossible to attend a party these days where there's not a tray of raw vegetables for munching. The idea is a great one, but too often it turns sour when stale, wilted veggies are used. There's nothing like a limp and soggy carrot baton to send even the most devoted dieter to the high-fat section of the table. Here are some secrets to serving vegetables in their prime:

- For fresh and lively produce, buy vegetables in season. In November, for instance, parsnips will be crisp and sweet, while asparagus is much less likely to be at its peak.
- Buy carrots with green tops attached. If the tops are bright and fresh, chances are the carrots haven't been sitting in a storeroom for months.
- Choose zucchini that's no longer than seven inches; it will be sweet and tender. Also, those with straight necks usually keep longer than their crooked-necked cousins.
- Create visual interest by serving both red and yellow cherry tomatoes. Pleasing the eye is as important as pleasing the palate.
- To get the most from snow peas, set them in a strainer and pour boiling water over them for about 5 seconds. The light blanching brings out the delicate flavors. Pat dry before serving.
- For an unusual twist, serve peeled and thinly sliced raw beets. Their taste is snappy and perfect with yogurt dill dips.

ROASTED SWEET PEPPER
DIPPING SAUCE

MAKES 1 CUP

3 roasted sweet red peppers (see page 84)
1 shallot, very finely minced
2 teaspoons olive oil
2 teaspoons freshly squeezed lemon juice
½ cup yogurt cheese (see pages 173 and 178)
*   or part-skim ricotta*

In a processor or blender combine the peppers, shallot, oil, and lemon juice; whiz until smooth. Fold in the cheese and serve with celery stalks, chunks of fresh fennel, plump shrimp, or whole-grain crackers.

Tops in Pops

Most of us know that air-popped popcorn, made without oil, is a better choice than that popped in oil. The challenge is to forgo the fat-filled butter topping. *Make* it easy to forget that fat by tossing warm popcorn with basil and finely grated parmesan, or with minced dried fruits like apricots and pears.

MAPLE-CINNAMON POPPED CORN

MAKES 8 CUPS

8 cups air-popped corn (use about 1/3 cup of kernels)
2 tablespoons maple syrup
1/2 teaspoon cinnamon

Preheat the oven to 200°F.

Combine the maple syrup and cinnamon in a small glass bowl and microwave, uncovered, on full power until very liquidy, about 20 seconds. If you don't have a microwave, heat the syrup in a small saucepan on the stovetop.

Pour the syrup over the popped corn and toss well to combine, making sure that all the pieces are coated. Then tip the popped corn onto a large cookie sheet with sides and spread it out. Bake for about 10 minutes, then turn off the oven and let the popcorn sit inside for about 30 minutes. Serve warm from the oven. Can be stored tightly covered for up to 2 days.

Nut butters like those made from peanuts, cashews, and almonds are rich, creamy, and low in saturated fat. Unfortunately, nut butters are high in calories. But you can easily cut those calories in half by combining equal parts of nut butter and water in a blender or processor and whizzing until smooth and emulsified. Use as you would any regular nut butter — on crackers and in sauces and dips.

SPICY PEANUT DIPPING SAUCE

MAKES ABOUT ¾ CUP

½ cup creamy peanut butter
½ cup water
½ teaspoon reduced-sodium soy sauce
¼ teaspoon hot pepper sauce, or to taste
½ teaspoon finely grated lime peel

Combine all the ingredients in a blender or processor and whiz until smooth and creamy. Great for dipping blanched snow peas, carrots, and cauliflower. Or try with bite-sized chunks of poached chicken.

Crash Course in Crackers

Check the nutritional information panel on the package. Many crackers, although appearing innocent, contain huge amounts of fat and sodium, while others—Scandinavian-type flat bread crackers, for example—are usually low in fat and high in fiber. Better yet—make your own!

CRISP PITA FANS

MAKES 32 CRACKERS

2 whole wheat pitas
2½ tablespoons olive oil

Preheat the oven to 400°F.

Use a kitchen shears to cut each pita into 8 triangles. Then open each triangle and cut in two—16 triangles for each pita.

Arrange the fans on a large cookie sheet crumbly side up; brush each fan with olive oil. Bake until crisp and light brown, about 12 minutes. Serve warm or at room temperature with lowfat cheeses or dipping sauces. Store tightly covered for up to 5 days.

Variations: After brushing on the oil, sprinkle with finely grated parmesan, minced fresh dill, or finely minced fresh garlic.

CROSTINI

4 slices good quality whole-grain bread

Preheat the oven to 400°F.

Cut each slice of bread into quarters and arrange them directly on a rack in the oven. Bake until crisp and browned, about 5 minutes.

Ideas for Serving Crostini

- Spread with a bean dip made from cooked white beans mashed with minced garlic and a splash of olive oil.
- Top with a lightly smoked sardine and a sprig of Italian parsley.
- Mix yogurt cheese with basil pesto and spread on warm crostini.

LEMON-LIMEADE SYRUP FOR REFRESHING BEVERAGES

1 cup white grape juice
½ cup sugar
juice and pulp of 4 lemons
juice and pulp of 4 limes

Combine the grape juice and sugar in a small saucepan and bring to a boil, stirring occasionally. Reduce the heat and simmer for about 5 minutes. Remove from heat and allow to cool.

Stir in the lemon and lime juice and pulp. Store refrigerated until ready to use.

For *lemon-limeade*: Stir 2 tablespoons of syrup into 1 cup of still or carbonated cold water and serve over ice. Garnish with a citrus twist or a mint sprig.

In the Club

Plain club soda and seltzer water are great mixers for making your own light sodas. Enjoy them as everyday thirst-quenchers or serve them as low-calorie party beverages. Here are some flavor ideas:

- Serve club soda on the rocks with a splash of bitters and a twist of lime.
- Mix equal parts of chilled club soda and orange juice and serve in champagne flutes.
- Pour a splash of exotic all-fruit juice (no-sugar-added) into a tall glass of seltzer. For instance, try papaya nectar or lingon-berry juice.
- Serve equal parts of pineapple juice and seltzer in chilled beer mugs.
- Brew and chill a colorful herbal tea, such as one made from hibiscus or rose hips. Then mix in equal parts with chilled seltzer and serve with a twist of lemon.
- Add a drop or two of vanilla extract to a tall glass of iced seltzer.

Getting Juiced

Buy low-sodium tomato juice and flavor it yourself with a splash of lemon juice. Tasters at the University of California at Berkeley thought that lightly salted and lemoned juices were equally tasty — and odds are you will, too.

TOMATO TODDY

2 SERVINGS

2 cups unsalted tomato juice
¼ teaspoon Worcestershire sauce
¼ teaspoon curry powder
pinch ground ginger

Combine all of the ingredients in a small saucepan and simmer until hot. Serve hot in warmed mugs.

HOT MULLED CIDER

MAKES 1 QUART

1 quart apple cider
3 whole cloves
3 whole allspice berries (whole allspice)
2 cinnamon sticks (about 2 inches long)
1 orange, sliced

Combine all of the ingredients in a large saucepan and simmer for at least an hour; strain; serve warm in heated mugs.

Variation: Instead of all cider, use 3 cups of cider and 1 cup of dry red wine.

Sparkling Teas

As we've cut back on high-calorie, high-fat beverages, we've found that some of the herbal teas make attractive alternatives. These herbal potions can be delicious and interesting, especially if they're combined creatively and brewed correctly. But it's a mistake, in our view, to think that one herb, or one flavor of anything for that matter, can be a satisfying experience. Here are some lively dried herb combinations and some tips on brewing:

- Lemongrass and spearmint, hot or cold
- Rose hips and blueberry leaf, hot or cold
- Rose petals, orange peel, and thyme, cold
- Raspberry leaf, peppermint, and ginger, hot or cold
- Lemon balm and peppermint, hot or cold

To *brew hot herbal tea,* use about 2 teaspoons of dried herb mixture for each cup of boiling water. Steep for 4 to 5 minutes, then strain and serve alone, with honey or citrus twists.

For *iced herbal teas,* prepare as you would hot teas, but double the amount of dried herbs to allow for melting ice.

Freeze herbal teas with sprigs of mint in ice cube trays and use to chill refreshing summer beverages.

The Grand Finale

Odds are this is the first chapter you turned to—and if you did, you aren't alone. Even when people begin to improve their diets, they still wonder, "What's for dessert?" Our answer is delicious cakes, cookies, pies, tarts, mousse, and frozen treats. What makes ours different is that not only are they tasty, they're also healthful. The secret is in the preparation.

Take cakes. A simple choice of the best-suited flour can let you reduce fat and sugar in a recipe without sacrificing tender texture. With a few modifications, pies can shed almost half their fat and calories and still maintain alluring flavors and aromas. Even cookies—those notoriously high-fat treats—bake beautifully without the usual dose of saturated fat.

As you may have suspected, fresh fruit figures into this dessert regime. You just need to know when fruits have the fullest flavors and which fruits taste creamy and rich without a trace of fat. Ready to learn?

MOIST CARROT CAKE

---

8 SERVINGS

½ cup (3 ounces) cup cake flour
⅓ cup brown sugar
1 teaspoon baking powder
½ teaspoon cinnamon
pinch salt
2 cups grated carrots (4–5 medium carrots)
¼ cup canola oil or vegetable oil

Preheat the oven to 350°F.

Into a medium bowl sift together the flour, sugar, baking powder, cinnamon, and salt. Add the carrots and oil; stir to combine.

Spray a 4½ x 8 ½-inch loaf pan with nonstick vegetable spray and scoop in the batter. Bake in the center of the oven for 20 to 25 minutes.

Let cool for about 5 minutes, then carefully turn the cake out onto a wire rack to cool completely. Slice and serve plain, or topped with a bit of all-fruit (no-sugar-added) apple butter.

Cake Recipes Revised

Here's how to turn your favorite cake recipes into healthful and delicious desserts:

- Substitute an equal amount of cake flour for the flour in your recipe. Cake flour is low in gluten and will give your cake a light and tender texture without the need for excess fat.
- Cut the fat by half. In other words, if the recipe calls for 1 cup of oil, use ½ cup instead, plus an additional ½ cup of skim milk, nonfat yogurt, or buttermilk.
- Slash the sugar. If you reduce the amount of fat in a cake and not the amount of sugar, the finished texture will be sticky. Plus, who needs the extra calories? In most recipes you can reduce the sugar by 25 percent without disturbing the structure of the cake. So if the recipe calls for 1 cup, use ¾ cup instead.
- Replace each whole egg with two egg whites.
- Pass up conventional frostings and icings in favor of more healthful cake toppings. Spread a lemon cake with an all-fruit preserve; top a piece of spice cake with lowfat vanilla yogurt; sprinkle a fruit cake with shaved dried papaya or apricots.

A *Healthful* Hint:

When baking, melt chocolate in the microwave, so it won't need large amounts of added butter to keep it from becoming grainy. Arrange chocolate pieces or chips in a small dish and microwave, uncovered, on medium power until the chocolate is just shiny. At this point it will be soft enough to stir until smooth.

BETTER BROWNIES

16 SMALL BROWNIES

These brownies are especially good sandwiched with all-fruit (no-sugar-added) raspberry jam or peanut butter.

2 ounces semi-sweet chocolate chips, melted
1 tablespoon margarine or butter, melted
⅓ cup quick oats
½ cup boiling water
½ cup cake flour
½ teaspoon baking powder
2 egg whites, beaten until frothy
⅓ cup dark brown sugar
1 teaspoon vanilla

Preheat the oven to 350°F.

In a small bowl combine the chocolate and butter or margarine; set aside to cool.

In a medium bowl combine the oats and water and let soak.

In a large bowl stir together the flour and baking powder. Pour in the egg whites, sugar, and vanilla, and continue to stir while you add in the chocolate and oats. *Don't overmix.*

Coat a 9 x 9-inch pan with nonstick vegetable spray and scoop in the batter. Bake until cooked through, about 18 minutes.

Set the pan on a rack to cool, then slice and serve.

Dark Secret

 Because brown sugar imparts more flavor than white, you can use less in cookie baking.

Never Say Diet

 Don't use diet margarine when you bake cookies: it contains water and will cause cookies to spread apart before they're baked through.

CINNAMON OAT COOKIES

MAKES ABOUT 18 COOKIES

2 tablespoons margarine (not dietetic)
  or sweet butter, softened
2 tablespoons nonfat yogurt
¼ cup brown sugar
1 egg white, beaten until bubbly
¼ cup (approximately 1½ ounces) unbleached flour
½ teaspoon baking soda
1 teaspoon cinnamon
¼ teaspoon finely grated lemon peel
¾ cup rolled oats

Preheat the oven to 400°F.

In a medium bowl combine the margarine or butter, yogurt, brown sugar, and egg white; beat until creamy with a hand mixer. (The mixture won't be emulsified, as in a high-fat cookie — and that's okay.)

Sift the flour, soda, and cinnamon into a medium bowl and stir in the lemon peel and oats. Pour in the wet mixture and combine well without overmixing.

Line a cookie sheet with parchment paper and drop the dough on in rounded teaspoonfuls. Bake until cooked through, about 8 to 10 minutes. Cool on a wire rack before serving; store in a tightly covered tin.

Smarter Cookies

When sticking cookies give you pause, don't resort to rubbing the baking sheet with fat. Instead, use parchment paper. Not only will it keep cookies from sticking, but parchment paper practically guarantees that the bottoms of your cookies won't burn. Also look for the new reusable baking liners. They perform the same functions and can be wiped clean and used indefinitely.

WHOLE WHEAT RAISIN COOKIES

MAKES ABOUT 2 DOZEN

2 tablespoons margarine (not dietetic) or sweet butter
2 tablespoons nonfat yogurt
1 egg white, beaten until frothy
3 tablespoons dark brown sugar
1 teaspoon vanilla extract
½ teaspoon baking soda
½ cup (approximately 2 ounces) unbleached flour
½ cup (approximately 2 ounces) whole wheat pastry flour
¼ cup raisins, chopped

Preheat the oven to 400°F.

Combine the margarine, yogurt, egg white, sugar, and vanilla in a medium bowl and use a hand mixer to combine well. (The mixture won't be emulsified, as in a high-fat cookie — and that's fine.)

Into a large bowl sift together the soda and flours. Then stir in the raisins. Scoop in the wet ingredients and combine well without overmixing.

Line a cookie sheet with parchment paper. Next, form rounded teaspoon-sized balls with the dough and arrange them on the sheet. Flatten a bit with the bottom of a glass and bake until cooked through, about 10 minutes.

Let the cookies cool on a wire rack. Store in a tightly covered tin.

Tea Time

 Flavored teas, like cinnamon, lemon and orange, add flavor without calories to baked goods. Use them in place of water or milk in pies, quick breads, muffins, and crisps.

SPICED PEACH CRISP

6 TO 8 SERVINGS

½ cup boiling spiced tea
⅓ cup quick oats
¾ cup whole wheat pastry flour
¾ teaspoon ginger
¾ teaspoon cinnamon
¼ teaspoon ground cloves
1 teaspoon baking powder
¼ teaspoon baking soda
2 tablespoons corn oil margarine or sweet butter, softened
½ cup molasses
1 egg white, beaten until frothy
1 pound (about 4 medium) peaches, peeled, pitted, and sliced
1 tablespoon finely ground toasted almonds

Preheat the oven to 350°F.

In a small bowl pour the tea over the oats; let them soak.

In a medium bowl stir together the flour, ginger, cinnamon, cloves, baking powder, and baking soda.

In a large bowl combine the margarine or butter, molasses, and egg white using a hand mixer. Then fold in the oat mixture and gradually fold in the flour mixture. *Don't overmix.*

Coat a 9-inch glass pie plate with nonstick vegetable spray and spread the peaches evenly on the bottom. Pour over the batter, sprinkle on the almonds, and bake until cooked through, about 25 to 30 minutes.

Let the crisp cool for about 10 minutes, then serve. Great with a scoop of vanilla ice milk or hot applesauce.

Variation: Substitute pears or apples in place of the peaches.

Cut the Crust

Turn a two-crust pie into a one-crust pie and you'll be saving fat and calories. For example, for an apple pie, line a pie tin with a thin bottom crust and scoop in the apple mixture. Cover with foil instead of a top pie crust and bake as usual.

STRAWBERRY TART

6 SERVINGS

½ cup whole wheat pastry flour
½ cup unbleached flour
2 tablespoons corn oil margarine or sweet butter, cut into pieces
½ cup lowfat cottage cheese
splash of water if necessary
1 cup lowfat vanilla yogurt
2 cups strawberries, halved
½ cup currant jelly

Preheat the oven to 375°F.

Combine the flours and margarine in a processor and whiz until the pieces of margarine are the size of cornmeal. With the motor running, scoop in the cottage cheese and continue to process until the mixture forms into a ball. If there's no ball after 6 seconds, pour in a splash of water and continue to process.

Spray a 10-inch tart pan with removable bottom with nonstick vegetable spray. Press in the dough, working it along the bottom and up the sides, until you have a smooth, even crust. Bake until golden and cooked through, about 25 minutes. Let the shell cool on a wire rack.

To fill, spread the yogurt over the bottom of the tart shell. Then arrange the berries over the yogurt. Meanwhile, melt the jelly in a small saucepan over low heat or in a small dish in the microwave, uncovered, on full power for about 30 seconds. Brush or spoon the melted jelly over the berries and chill for at least an hour before serving.

Perfecting the Pie

If you have a favorite high-fat pie that you just can't give up, make it into a tart instead. Since tart pans are shallower than pie tins, you'll be eating less while enjoying your old favorite. Cutting the recipe for the filling in half and using a 9- or 10-inch tart pan will usually do the trick.

CHEESECAKE TART

8 SERVINGS

4 ounces graham crackers
2 tablespoons margarine or butter, melted
2 cups lowfat cream cheese or cottage cheese
1 egg
1 teaspoon vanilla extract
¼ teaspoon almond extract
2 tablespoons sugar
fresh berries for garnish

Preheat the oven to 325°F.

For the crust:
Combine the crackers and margarine in a processor and whiz until crumbly. Spray a 9-inch tart pan with removable bottom with nonstick vegetable spray and press in the crumbs. Don't forget to go up the sides.

For the filling:
Combine the cream cheese, egg, extracts, and sugar in the processor; whiz until smooth.

Pour the cheese mixture into the tart shell and bake until firm, about 30 minutes. Serve very slightly chilled, garnished with the berries.

Savor the Flavor

Flavored coffees make interesting and fragrant no-calorie desserts. For instance, try toasted almond, hazelnut, or Irish cream. Be sure to buy pure coffee and not the instant kind that comes with sugar and fat added.

PUMPKIN PIE WITH MAPLE-WALNUT CRUST

8 SERVINGS

1¼ cups whole wheat pastry flour
¼ cup canola oil or vegetable oil
1 tablespoon maple syrup
1 teaspoon black walnut extract
1 tablespoon unflavored gelatin
¼ cup apple juice
1¼ cup or 10 ounces canned cooked pumpkin puree
½ cup evaporated skim milk
1 whole egg, beaten
2 egg whites, beaten until bubbly
½ cup brown sugar
½ teaspoon cinnamon
1 teaspoon vanilla extract
1 tablespoon dark rum

Preheat the oven to 375°F.

For the crust:
Combine the flour, oil, maple syrup, and extract in a processor and whiz until you have a smooth ball. Press the dough into the bottom and sides of a lightly oiled 9-inch glass pie dish, and bake until dry, about 20 to 25 minutes. Let cool before filling.

For the filling:
Combine the gelatin and juice in a small dish; set aside. Combine the pumpkin, milk, egg, egg whites, sugar, and cinnamon in a medium saucepan; heat on medium. Stir frequently until

thickened, then add the gelatin, vanilla, and rum and stir until well combined and heated through.

Pour the pumpkin mixture into the pie shell and chill overnight before serving.

PINK GRAPEFRUIT MOUSSE

6 SERVINGS

Delicious with Whole Wheat Raisin Cookies, page 188.

1 tablespoon unflavored gelatin
¼ cup white grape juice
6 ounces pink grapefruit juice concentrate
¼ cup sugar
1 cup skim milk or evaporated skim milk

In a small bowl combine the gelatin and grape juice and let soften for about 5 minutes.

Combine the grapefruit juice concentrate and sugar in a small saucepan and stir in the gelatin. Simmer until the gelatin has dissolved, about 2 minutes. Then let the mixture cool for about 20 minutes.

Stir in the milk and let chill until firm, about 2 hours.

Fiber-filled fruits can help you feel fuller, which is great if you're watching your weight. For the boldest flavors without added sugar, choose fruits that are in season and combine them with other fruits to make salads that come alive with taste and color. Enjoy these combinations:

Spring

- Sliced strawberries, chopped apricots, and fresh blueberries, tossed with freshly squeezed lime juice
- Chunked pineapple, tangerine sections, and sliced bananas, tossed with plain yogurt and minced fresh mint

Summer

- Chunked cantaloupe and watermelon with sliced strawberries, sprinkled with granola
- Sliced peaches and red raspberries, splashed with amaretto

Autumn

- Seedless grapes, chopped pecans, and sliced tart apples, tossed with cinnamon and cider
- Sliced pears and pitted cherries, tossed with lemon yogurt

Winter

- Chopped apples and plums, tossed with raisins and a splash of maple syrup
- Orange sections in cognac, sprinkled with crushed macaroons

QUICK DIP FOR FRESH FRUITS

For dessert in a flash, serve this dip with sliced apples, pears, peaches, or nectarines. Keep the fruit from browning by tossing it with a bit of lime juice.

½ cup plain nonfat yogurt
2 ounces lowfat cream cheese
1 tablespoon brown sugar
¼ teaspoon finely grated fresh ginger
¼ teaspoon finely grated lemon peel

Combine all of the ingredients in a processor or blender and whiz until just smooth. Serve at room temperature or very slightly chilled with an array of fresh fruit.

Creamy without the Cream

When preparing ice milks or other frozen treats, let the base chill overnight before proceeding with the recipe. The texture of the final product will be creamier — without a drop of added cream!

STRAWBERRY ICE MILK

MAKES ABOUT A QUART

2 cups skim milk
1 egg, beaten
¼ cup sugar
2 cups strawberries, pureed

Combine the milk, egg, and sugar in a medium saucepan and heat on medium, whisking frequently. Continue to heat until the mixture thickens enough to coat the back of a spoon, about 15 minutes. Then let the mixture chill in the refrigerator overnight.

Combine the chilled milk mixture with the berries and process in an ice cream maker according to manufacturer's instructions. If you're not going to serve the ice milk immediately, freeze it, but plan to let it soften for about 20 minutes before you serve it.

An Apple a Day...

This old wives' tale may have some merit. Apples contain pectin, a type of fiber thought to reduce levels of harmful cholesterol. When eaten along with other fruits, vegetables, beans, and grains rich in cholesterol-lowering fiber, the apple is part of a team that can make a real difference.

BAKED APPLE COMPOTE

6 SERVINGS

Great sprinkled with granola or topped with lowfat vanilla yogurt.

*4 large baking apples
  (Stayman and Rome are a nice combination),
  peeled, cored, and chunked
juice and pulp of ½ lemon
1 tablespoon flour
¼ teaspoon cinnamon
¼ teaspoon freshly grated nutmeg
2 tablespoons brown sugar*

Preheat the oven to 450°F.

Toss all of the ingredients into a 9-inch (not deep) glass pie dish and combine well. Cover with foil and bake until the apples are tender and fragrant, about 30 minutes. Serve warm or very slightly chilled.

Many tropical fruits have smooth and creamy textures reminiscent of more fattening treats. Pureed mango, banana, and papaya, for instance, are rich and silky without a trace of fat. Stir them into ice milks or yogurts before freezing, or use them as a base for sauces for cakes and fresh fruit.

FROZEN BANANA YOGURT

MAKES ABOUT A QUART

1 pound (about 3 medium) peeled and sliced bananas
juice and pulp of ½ lemon
⅓ cup brown sugar
¼ teaspoon cinnamon
2 cups plain nonfat yogurt

Combine the bananas, lemon, sugar, and cinnamon in a processor or blender; whiz until smooth. Then fold in the yogurt and process in an ice cream maker according to manufacturer's directions. If you're not serving the yogurt immediately, freeze it — but plan to let it soften at room temperature for about 20 minutes before serving.

Making It Creamy

When it comes to lowfat frozen desserts, there's no substitute for an ice cream maker for keeping the textures smooth and creamy. If you don't have one, try to pick one up. They range in price from $25 to $500.

PEACH AND PAPAYA FREEZE

MAKES ABOUT 1 QUART

2 cups (about a pound) peeled, pitted, and pureed peaches
2 cups (1 large papaya) peeled and seeded papaya
2 tablespoons freshly squeezed lemon juice
1/3 cup sugar

Combine all of the ingredients in a processor or blender and whiz until smooth. Then process in an ice cream maker according to the manufacturer's directions. If you're not going to serve immediately, freeze it — but plan to let it soften for about 20 minutes before serving.

MELON SORBET

This sorbet makes great frozen pops, too.

  ½ cup apple juice
  2 tablespoons sugar
  2 pounds red watermelon, seeded and chopped

Combine the juice and sugar in a small saucepan and bring to a boil. Place in a small glass or microwave bowl in the microwave until the sugar has dissolved, about 2 minutes. Either way, let the syrup cool to room temperature.

Meanwhile, puree the melon in a processor or blender. Stir in the syrup and process in an ice cream maker according to manufacturer's directions. If you're not going to serve the sorbet immediately, freeze it — but plan to let it soften for about 15 minutes before serving.

Dandy Candy

Freeze blueberries and seedless grapes. Then eat without defrosting instead of candy. They're sweet and tasty and contain a fraction of candy's calories.

MANGO SAUCE

MAKES ABOUT 1½ CUPS

1 large ripe mango
juice and pulp of 1 lime
1 tablespoon brown sugar
1 tablespoon margarine or sweet butter

Peel the mango over a blender container to catch the juices. Then slice in the meat of the fruit, discarding the stone. Add the lime, sugar, and margarine; whiz until smooth.

Scoop the mixture into a small saucepan and heat on medium-high, stirring frequently, until fragrant and slightly thickened, about 5 minutes. Serve warm over cake or chilled over fruits such as bananas and grapes.

Index

Toast, English Muffin, 6
Frozen Desserts, 196, 198–200
  Frozen Banana Yogurt, 198
  Melon Sorbet, 200
Peach and Papaya Freeze, 199
Strawberry Ice Milk, 196
Fruit (s), 2
  beverages, with club soda, 179
  Cottage Cheese Pancakes with,
    7
  Compote, with Ginger and
    Lime, 14
  dried, 14
  fiber in, 28
  Quick Dip for, 195
  in salads, 60
  salads, 194
  shakes, 28-30
  spreads, 27
  as sweeteners, 9
  Swiss-Mixed Breakfast Sundae,
    12
  tropical toppings, 198
Frying, 161

G

Game, 140
Gammelost cheese, 173
Garlic, 32
  Fragrant Shrimp Soup with
    Ginger and, 44
  Greens with, 83
  -Grilled Chicken, 99
  Leg of Lamb with Rosemary,
    Currants and, 141
  Roasted, 171
  -Tomato Sauce, Ribs with, 138
Ginger, 32
  Dried Fruit Compote with, 14
  -Glazed Fresh Tuna, 111

-Lemon Chicken, 93, 95
  sauce for vegetables, 89
  Shrimp Soup with Garlic and,
    44
Golden Onion-Dill Bread, 22
Grains
  as side dish, 71
  in soups, 40
Grapefruit Mousse, 193
Grapes, 12
  frozen, 201
  in fruit salad, 194
  juice, Three-Fruit Cooler, 29
  in salads, 60
Great Northern Bean Sandwich,
    63
Great Valley Mills, 1
Green beans, 40
  sauce for, 89
  Yard-long, 91
Greens, 83
  with Garlic, 83
  sautéed, 68
  shopping for, 49–50
Gremolata, 122
Grilled
  Chicken, 49, 99
    with Garlic, 99
  Fish, 112
  Mahi Mahi Brochettes, 113
  Monkfish, 112
  Mushroom Brochettes, 172
  Squash, 87
  Turkey Steak, 107
  Vegetables, 87
Grouper
  Cold Poached, with Red Onion
    and Dill, 120
  with Mexican Vinaigrette, 119
Guacomole, 123
Gumbo, Chicken, 42

H

Haddock
  Bouillabaisse Salad, 126
  Cold Poached, with Red Onion
    and Dill, 120
  with Mexican Vinaigrette, 119
  New Orleans, with Chili Sauce
    and Spaghetti, 128
  in Packet, 114
  with Vermouth and Herbs, 115
Halibut
  Ginger-Glazed, 111
  Grilled, 112
  Pan-Grilled with Frizzled
    Onions, 110
Hazelnut oil, 51
Herb(s), 33, 151
  Creamy French Dressing, 52
  Flounder with Vermouth and,
    115
  in salads, 57
  Teas, 179, 181, 189
  Tempeh with Vegetables and,
    164
Horseradish and Onion relish, 90
Hot
  Cereal Mix, 13
  Mulled Cider, 180
  Tomato Toddy, 180
Hot pepper sauce, 127

I

Ice cream maker, 199
Ice Milk, Strawberry, 196

J

Jalapeño, 137
  Corn Bread Pudding with, 5

Jamaican Jerk Pork, 137
Jicama, 91
Juice, 6, 9

K

Kale
  Autumn Salad, 57
  Fettuccini with, 152
  with Garlic, 83
  in soups, 44

L

Lamb
  Chops with Curry Butter, 142
  Leg, with Rosemary, Garlic
    and Currants, 141
Lasagne, 147
Leeks, 33
  Braised, with Roasted Red
    Peppers, 84
  Soup, 35
    with Fresh Tomato, 37
  steamed, julienned, 110
Lemon
  -Ginger Chicken, 93, 95
  Light and Tender Waffles, 10
  Limeade Syrup, 178
  Sauce
    for shellfish, 122-123
    for vegetables, 89
  sautéing with, 90
  in soup stock, 32, 34
  Zucchini Quick Bread, 18
Lentil Puree with Roasted
    Chicken, 45
Lettuce, 52
  red leaf, 50
  Sandwiches, 63

R

Raisin(s), 11, 12
  Cracked Wheat Cinnamon
    Bread, 16
  -Orange Buttermilk Oatcakes, 8
  Whole Wheat Cookies, 188
Raspberry
  Blender Breakfast, 28
  fruit salad, 194
  Preserves, 27
Red pepper
  Braised Leeks with Roasted, 84
  and Chili sauce for corn, 89
  and Corn
    Soufflé, 165
    Summer Salad, 56
  Roasted Sweet, 84
    Dipping Sauce, 174
  Salad, 56
    with Walnut Vinaigrette, 51
  and Sweet Potato relish, 90
Red snapper
  Braised Chinese Style, 117
  Cold Poached, with Red Onion
    and Dill, 120
  with Mexican Vinaigrette, 119
  in Packet, 114
  whole, 121
Relish
  Sweet Potato, 90
  Onion and Horseradish, 90
Ribs with Garlic Tomato Sauce,
  138
Rice(s), 75–76
  Arborio, 76
  Aromatic, 76
  and Beans with Toasted Pine
    Nuts, 77
  blends, 162

brown, 46, 76
  buying, 76
  Curried Dressing, 75
Crust, Savory, 160
long-grain, 76
medium-grain, 76
Pilaf, 72
Risotto with Tiny White Beans
  and Peas, 163
short-grain, 76
in soup, 40
Turkey Soup with Saffron and,
  46
Unfried, Chinese Style, 162
whole flaked brown, 12
Wild, Vegetable Soup with, 40
Ricotta cheese, 5, 147
  and pasta toss, 150
  Sandwich with Tomato, 63
Rigatoni, 146
  with Tomato Sauce and Blue
    Cheese, 156
Risotto with Tiny White Beans
  and Peas, 163
Rosemary
  Crisp Potatoes with, 79
  Leg of Lamb with Garlic,
    Currants and, 141
  Roast Duck with Vermouth
    and, 104
Rotini, 146
Roux, Healthful, 41
Rye and Caraway Flatbread, 23

S

Saffron, 46
  Chicken Cutlets with Green
    Olives and, 102
  Turkey Soup with Rice and, 46

cracked, 16
fiber and, 16
germ, 7, 9, 16
See also Whole wheat
White Bean(s)
Eggplant Soup with Tiny, 38
Risotto with Peas and, 163
Salad with Orange-Cider
Dressing, 54
Whole grain(s), 2
breads, pan for, 18
flakes, 12
Whole wheat
hot cereal with, 13
Raisin Cookies, 188
shells, 146
Wild Rice, Fresh Vegetable Soup
with, 40
Wine
adding, to soup, 32, 41
in Demi-Glace, 34
Mulled, 180
Winter salad, 57
fruit, 194
Winter squash, 40, 57, 71
salad, 57
Wire racks, 21

Y

Yard-long beans, 91
Yeast, 22

Yogurt
Breakfast
shakes, 28–30
Swiss-Mixed Sundae, 12
Cheese, 173, 178
Dip for Fruit, 195
Frozen Banana, 198
Horseradish relish, 90
Salad dressing
Autumn, 57
Spring, 56
Sauces
Caraway, 89
Chili, 122
Chutney, 123
Curry, 122
Dill and Lemon, 89
Dilled, for chicken, 101
Herbed, for shellfish, 123
Soup, Avocado-Cucumber, 35
Sour Cream substitute, 80

Z

Zucchini, 174
Grilled, 87
-Lemon Quick Bread, 18
and pasta toss, 150
Puree with Toasted Cumin, 39
Salad, 51
Sautéed in Tomato Juice, 90
Tempeh with Herbs and, 164